The TRIUNE GOD *and* MISSION

The Triune God and Mission

A Theology of Mission

PIETER VERSTER

Foreword by A. van de Beek

WIPF & STOCK · Eugene, Oregon

THE TRIUNE GOD AND MISSION
A Theology of Mission

Copyright © 2022 Pieter Verster. All rights reserved. Except for brief quotations in critical publications or reviews, no part of this book may be reproduced in any manner without prior written permission from the publisher. Write: Permissions, Wipf and Stock Publishers, 199 W. 8th Ave., Suite 3, Eugene, OR 97401.

Wipf & Stock
An Imprint of Wipf and Stock Publishers
199 W. 8th Ave., Suite 3
Eugene, OR 97401

www.wipfandstock.com

PAPERBACK ISBN: 978-1-6667-3625-0
HARDCOVER ISBN: 978-1-6667-9435-9
EBOOK ISBN: 978-1-6667-9436-6

JUNE 13, 2022 8:17 AM

Scripture quotations marked (NIV) are taken from the Holy Bible, New International Version®, NIV®. Copyright © 1973, 1978, 1984, 2011 by Biblica, Inc.™ Used by permission of Zondervan. All rights reserved worldwide. www.zondervan.com The "NIV" and "New International Version" are trademarks registered in the United States Patent and Trademark Office by Biblica, Inc.™

I dedicate this book to my wife Ernéne Roalda Verster (née Uÿs).
All my love!

Contents

Foreword: A Real Message to the World | ix
    by A. van de Beek

Preface | xiii

Acknowledgments | xv

Background and Viewpoints | 1

Jesus, Son of God, Is Our Atonement | 19

Exegetic and Hermeneutic Considerations
Regarding the Glory of Jesus Christ as Our Redeemer | 31

The Three Offices of Jesus Christ | 43

The Holy Spirit | 68

The Holy Spirit as the Spirit of Revelation,
the Spirit of Life, and the Cosmological Work of the Spirit | 86

The Implications of the Person and Work of the Holy Spirit | 101

God as the Father in His Love and Glory | 117

God the Father, Jesus the Son:
Love, the Holy Spirit, and Mission | 135

Bibliography | 141

Subject Index | 151

Scripture Index | 155

Foreword

A Real Message to the World

A. van de Beek

Mission was mainly winning souls for a long time. The church often operated as a company that tries to increase its market share. Certainly, missionaries were inspired by true love for people and wanted to save them, not only for eternal life but also from poverty and diseases. However, the overall focus of mission was on church growth, and this more quantitatively than qualitatively. Mission was about numbers.

The twentieth century displays a fully different approach. Mission is not about quantitative growth of the church, but its horizon is the world, and increasingly the whole creation. God's salutary work is not focused on the church but directed to the world. The movement of mission is not absorbing people from the world into the church as an exclusive community with strong borders, but proclaiming the good message of God's love and his renewing work to the world. Pneumatology increasingly joined Christology, and subsequently the love of the Creator to his creation became the new paradigm for mission. Mission does not serve ecclesiastic exclusivism but is inclusive for all human beings and the whole creation. This also includes human traditions and the large variety of contexts wherein they operate.

Verster fully supports this turn. His focus is the world. However, he makes a next step: the world is not as it should be. This is precisely the message implied in the coming of Christ. It does not affirm what is occurring in the world. It does not accept any tradition and any context. On the contrary, the message of the gospel is a critical message. A message which only confirms what is present is not at all a message. It is certainly not a salutary message. It only supports the status quo. The message which is the content of Christian mission as *missio Dei* disturbs the status quo. Its center is the crucified Christ: a person who was executed by the political and religious leaders of his time because of his critical message and behavior. Proclaiming the gospel of Christ is proclaiming the sin of the world with its unjust structures, even more with its selfish interests and exploitation of dependent people, and of the whole creation.

It is this critical message which Verster brings to the fore. The light of the gospel is for the whole world, but not by accepting all people as they are and any tradition as it is, but by unmasking people in their egoism and greed, their injustice and exploitation. Mission is a prophetic work in the Spirit of the prophetic presence of Christ in the world. Verster stresses that the Spirit is the Spirit of Christ. When that relation is not continuously guarded, mission soon becomes uncritical because pneumatology is filled in with human self-affirming interests. The coming of Christ, as *missio Dei*, is the core of the missionary task of the church when she is involved in this divine mission. And the center of Christ's coming is his death on the cross in his priestly service to the world.

It is in the power of the Spirit that this message is proclaimed in the world—and this divine power is needed because this message confronts the powers which rule the world and its history. Consequently, they will oppose it. But precisely therefore it is a liberating message to the people who are oppressed by these powers. Justice of God is proclaimed in an unjust world. Verster extensively elaborates the work of Christ and the relation of the Spirit to him, more than is usual in modern missiological works, which often focus on the world and contextual issues. However, this new concentration on the core of Christian faith and on the content of the missionary message is needed, for otherwise mission runs the risk of becoming uncritical and with its focus on the world just to confirm the world as it is—as a soft movement which does not consider the weight of sin and accordingly has no liberating message for those who suffer by it.

Verster's book is a much-needed critical scholarly contribution to missiology today. The way he operates methodologically makes it even more valuable. He does not take on his position in order to subsequently criticize those who have a different opinion. On the contrary, he searches for what is valuable in the work of other theologians and brings it together for his positive discourse. So he joins people who are far away in the sociogram of theology. This is another merit of the book: breaking down walls which theologians have erected around their own bubble and merging thoughts which seemed to exclude each other.

BRAM VAN DE BEEK
Emeritus Professor of the Vrije Universiteit van Amsterdam

Preface

PIETER VERSTER is a Research Fellow at the University of the Free State. Prior to his retirement, he was professor in missiology in the Faculty of Theology and Religion, University of the Free State. He was awarded a C3 grading by the National Research Foundation (NRF). He is also an ordained minister of the Dutch Reformed Church. In 2008, Edwin Mellen Press, New York, published his book *A Theology of Christian Missions: What Should the Church Seek to Accomplish?* Sun Press published two of his books: *New Hope for the Poor* (2012) and *Jesus Christ, Seun van God, is ons versoening: 'n Missionêre Christologie* (2017). Besides writing a number of academic articles, he also produced popular books and articles and delivered papers at various local and international congresses.

This current publication is based on research funded by the South African National Research Foundation (NRF). All opinions, conclusions, and proposals are those of the author, for which the NRF does not accept any responsibility.

This edition is also based on the following publications in Afrikaans: *Jesus Christ, Seun van God, is ons versoening: 'n Missionêre Christologie* and *Die wonderbare Heilige Gees én die Vader van liefde: 'n Missionêre teologie*.

It is essential to proclaim the Trinity as the essential basis for all mission. The theology of mission is a wonderful confession of the love and glory of the Triune God. In this world of terrible destruction and want, the love of God in Jesus Christ should be proclaimed. Only in him is there salvation. This salvation is complete because he is God of God, Light of Light, very God of very God. Athanasius's glorious confession should be acknowledged. It always played an important role in his theology.

The Holy Spirit, as the Spirit of Christ, brings complete salvation in Christ. He glorifies Jesus Christ; he facilitates faith, and he institutes the church. The Holy Spirit is, therefore, totally unique and wonderful. It is

Preface

essential that mission lives from the Spirit and as such recognizes Jesus Christ as Lord. This complements the witness that the Father shows eternal love in his Son Jesus Christ. Now that theology emulates the spirit of the times, we must unequivocally testify to the power of the Spirit that Jesus is Lord and that the Father is the Father of love. Central to this is Jesus Christ's death on the cross and resurrection, as confirmed by the Holy Spirit. This is often an attempt to stem the tide, but we must unequivocally testify to it.

Acknowledgments

My heartfelt thanks to Mrs. Ronel Ellis, for hours of typing; to Mrs. Marie-Thérèse Murray and Mrs. Huibré Lombard, for their competent language editing; to Profs. Cas Vos, Bram van de Beek, Andries Snyman, Piet Strauss, Maniraj Sukdaven, Dr. André Odendaal, and Dr. Henco van der Westhuizen for their extremely valuable input. Dr. Wessel Wessels, ministers Adrie Potgieter (Els) and Bongani Ngesi kindly helped with the research. I am personally responsible for suggestions and conclusions as well as for any errors.

To my wife, Ernéne Roalda, all my love and appreciation for years of support. My children Wanda, son-in-law Wilhelm Odendaal, and Frida and Pieter Lafras, many thanks for all your support and love.

I also thank Liezel Meintjies and SunBonani Publishers for previous editions.

I highly appreciate the financial support by the University of the Free State and the National Research Foundation (NRF). The SA Academy of Science and Arts provided generous financial support for the Afrikaans edition of the Christology. This book is my own view and the UFS, NRF, and SAAWK should not be held responsible in any way of views expressed.

My sincere thanks to both the Department of Practical and Missional Theology and the Faculty of Theology and Religion for their continuous support.

All honor to the Father, the Son, and the Holy Spirit.
Soli Deo Gloria.

Background and Viewpoints

INTRODUCTION

This work is a theology of mission. This means that a theological approach is used. Bosch explains in detail what he understands by "mission as theology."[1] He points out that there is a shift of theology of mission to missionary theology. Initially, mission was understood exclusively as the saving of souls or the expansion of the church. The question was: How can we execute this task? This was, however, viewed as something that must simply be added. Bosch points out that, by the sixth decade of the previous century, it was generally accepted that mission belongs to the essence of the church.[2] The church is not simply against the world, but it is sent into the world for the sake of the world. Mission is thus viewed not merely as an activity of the church, but as the nature of the church.[3] According to Bosch, this means that mission also includes all aspects of the incarnation.[4] Trinitarian mission is thus more than the church. God loves the world as a whole. All aspects of sinful humanity must thus be taken into account.[5] Theologizing also means that all aspects of theology must include mission as agenda. Theology must always include a dimension of mission and convey the specifics of mission. Missiology must constantly challenge the theological disciplines to be *theologia viatorum*, to reflect on the way of the gospel through the world. This must always be done critically on our own

---

1. Bosch, *Transforming Mission*, 492–93.
2. Bosch, *Transforming Mission*, 492–93.
3. Bosch, *Transforming Mission*, 493.
4. Bosch, *Transforming Mission*, 493.
5. Bosch, *Transforming Mission*, 494.

interpretations of missiology. Faith remains non-negotiable.[6] The issue of praxis is, however, also very important. Currently, there is the danger that context becomes all-defining. One must guard against complete subjectivism. It is essential to fully consider the context.[7]

From a theological perspective, I am convinced that a confessional approach best addresses the current challenges. It is still important to practice confessional theology from the confessions of faith in order to allow Scripture to talk in the unity of faith. Confessional theology also arises from the heart of the church. One should also regard the historical link with the church in the past. The church has existed for ages, and the confessions bind the church over the ages. Confessional theology binds the church in the history of the church. It is obvious that the deductive method, where the confession is inferred from Scripture, is still essential for sound theology. No theology can be neutral. Theology can reflect on current issues as it is directed by classical confessions. The confessions have dealt with the major questions of the time, resulting in the ability to address the new demands. In this instance, Calvin's handling of Scripture is very important.[8] Not only does he confirm the truth of the revelation in Scripture, but he also points to the nonbelievers' denial thereof. Scripture speaks, and the truth is confirmed through the Word. This truth of the Word can be confessed. What is more essential, especially nowadays, than the issue of Christ's deity and God's omnipotence in Nicaea? The consolation of Dordt also applies to the need and anxiety of modern man. The Heidelberg Catechism's Question and Answer 1 is essential. Of course, new questions and problems must be approached from this angle. The principle of *sola scriptura* must be complied with, but the profound insights of the confessions unlock doors for this. Although modern-day challenges require new thoughts and in-depth reflection, they can also be addressed by means of the deductive method of confessional theology. Scripture offers in-depth answers to the questions on life and death, humaneness amid suffering, eternal life amid issues about God's promises. One must guard against current theologizing and allow Scripture to talk in the confessional approach. For example, Heyns and Jonker explain how the confessions as *repetitio Sacrae Scripturae* confirm confessional theology.[9]

---

6. Bosch, *Transforming Mission*, 496–97.
7. Bosch, *Transforming Mission*, 498.
8. Calvin, *Institusie*, 1.vi.1.
9. Heyns and Jonker, *Op Weg met die Teologie*, 213.

Based on this recognition, it is clear that God exists and that he is concerned about the human being, including the human being in the present world's challenges of post-modernism, decolonization, and the fourth Industrial Revolution. Van den Berg refers to the ways in which one thinks about God on social media.[10] There are even tweets about God. One must be aware that the specific revelation must determine in detail revelation in general.

First, the hermeneutic and exegetic premises must be established. The premises in the approach of Trinitarian theology must be fixed. The basis of the study must thus be explained. In theological reflection, one must inquire about the content of the scientific view and follow the reformatory approach. This implies that the conviction that God reveals himself forms the basis of theology. Van der Walt writes that, already since its beginning, Christian religion was viewed not as an escape from the world but rather as a world-changing transformative power.[11] Life as a whole must be renewed. The inner life must determine the relationship to God and the relationship to our fellow human being and the rest of creation.[12]

God reveals himself in his full glory through Scripture, the *sola scriptura* principle. As a rule, it is not always clear how Scripture talks. The reformatory approach always wants to take the entire spectrum of interpretation seriously, but it still confirms that Scripture conveys God's revelation.

In general, the meaning of Scripture determines the interpretation. A continuous thread underlies the revelation of God despite the numerous voices. One should thus not ignore that *sacra scriptura sui ipsius interpres est* (sacred Scripture interprets itself) is a hermeneutic key for God's recognizable revelation.

Migliore stresses the irreplaceability of the Bible as the source that binds the living God, revealed in Jesus Christ, to man by the strength of the Holy Spirit.[13] Christians do not believe in the Bible; they believe in God who is proclaimed in the Bible. For this reason, the Bible is the unique witness of the sovereign grace of God that is visible in the history of Israel, but especially in the life, death, and resurrection of Jesus Christ. Migliore further confirms that the witness of Scripture is polyphonic

---

10. Van den Berg, "Tweeting God: Christian Motifs," 174; Van den Berg, "Tweeting God: Everyday Life."

11. Van der Walt, *Visie op die Werklikheid*, 1.

12. Van der Walt, *Visie op die Werklikheid*, 1.

13. Migliore, *Faith Seeking Understanding*, 50.

rather than homophonic.[14] The Bible's wealthy insights are also extraordinary. Migliore writes,

> The Bible is a witness, and at its centre it attests the sovereign, liberating grace of God in Christ. As described by the biblical narratives, God is always greater than we imagine. Scripture not only declares the coming of the Christ but tells the story of the crucified Christ; it not only praises the eternally rich God but proclaims that this God became one of the poor; it not only speaks of God's judgment and grace but declares that God stands on the side of the poor and the oppressed and judges the exalted and the powerful. This is the ever-disturbing, even revolutionary witness of the Bible.[15]

In terms of the principles according to which the Bible must be explained, Migliore provides the following guidelines:

1. Historical and literary sensitivity is required, without failing to appreciate the unique witness concerning the living God.
2. Scripture must be interpreted from a theocentric angle. The witness concerning the Triune God, namely the God of Israel who comes to us in Jesus Christ through the strength of the Holy Spirit, must be confirmed.
3. Scripture must be interpreted from a church perspective, within the context of witnesses of the church.
4. Scripture must also be interpreted contextually.[16]

Berkhof pointed out that Scripture is the fruit of God's revelation.[17] For this reason, the scriptural documents attest to the revelation to Israel and in Christ. The way in which the Bible is interpreted is closely linked to the question as to the authority of Scripture that must be viewed as a concept of "meeting."[18] As the relation between revelation and Scripture is indirect, the authority of Scripture is also indirect. Scripture mediates the meeting with God.[19] A text-oriented approach is followed to determine the

---

14. Migliore, *Faith Seeking Understanding*, 51.
15. Migliore, *Faith Seeking Understanding*, 52.
16. Migliore, *Faith Seeking Understanding*, 53–63.
17. Berkhof, *Christelijk Geloof*, 82.
18. Berkhof, *Christelijk Geloof*, 91.
19. Berkhof, *Christelijk Geloof*, 93.

person and work of Christ, the Holy Spirit, and the Father for mission. One must recognize that various approaches also address the Trinity, but in this instance the Bible in all its aspects is taken as starting point. When taking the general revelation into account, other, wider aspects will certainly have to be addressed, but always in light of specific revelation. According to the exegetic approach, however, the text must always be analyzed against the background of that time. It will be acceptable to refer to a few texts if they are evaluated from the specific background and genre by also referring to commentaries and to both biblical and systematic theologies. This emphasizes that the Holy Spirit has inspired Scripture, so that the *sola scriptura* is extremely important.

PROBLEMATICS OF POSTMODERNISM

The champions of postmodernism find it difficult to talk about basic truths and the admission of truths. Alfsvåg explains that the Christian missionary was viewed as someone who stands for and represents the truth.[20] This is currently being questioned, because the concept of "truth" is changeable. One must strive towards accepting the other, thus dismissing the exclusion of those who do not know the "truth." He refers to Derrida and Caputo, who dismiss the finality and definability of the concept of "truth."[21] Derrida uses the concept of "difference" to show that there is a difference between what is meant and what is said. It is, however, possible to overcome the relativity of interpretations, thus enabling religious interpretation. Both Derrida and Caputo criticize the one-sided modern definition of rationality. An important question is: Where does one seek the realization of the good if there is no absolute? Denial of the absolute leads to absolutization of the human subject.[22]

According to the postmodernists, the principles of creation, the fall, redemption, and the end of time are no longer tenable. There are no "grand narratives." Scripture must, therefore, also question itself and be deconstructed. The old image of the world is gone, and the new scientific image of the world leaves no room for creation as projected in the Bible; less so for the fall, and less so for redemption as a substitute. It must, however, be pointed out that one must acknowledge the dynamics of Scripture, read

20. Alfsvåg, "Postmodern Epistemology," 54.
21. Alfsvåg, "Postmodern Epistemology," 56.
22. Alfsvåg, "Postmodern Epistemology," 60.

in terms of the specific nature of Scripture, that should not be viewed as a scientific text, but rather as essential truths about God, creation, and redemption.

Alfsvåg's solution is that the story of Jesus Christ, who is present as Gift and Giver at Holy Communion, enables us to trust God and to confirm that God is the Giver of all that is good.[23] To confirm the integrity of the Christian story does not mean that those who support other stories should be treated with violence, but rather that the telling and retelling of the Christian story forms the basis of Christian mission.

THE REFORMATORY PRINCIPLE

From a reformatory perspective, the truths of Scripture still prevail. One must acknowledge the text's unique nature and truth. The text and its many possibilities provide guidelines for understanding God's revelation. The likelihood that God himself speaks in Scripture is based on Scripture as such and on the faith that accepts this liberating truth. God reveals himself and conveys his truth, which is closely associated with the evidence in Scripture itself. The source text confirms what is visible. In this respect, the Belgic Confession of Faith confesses that God is indeed revealed and recognizable in Scripture, that God is recognizable in Scripture through the working of the Holy Spirit.[24] God reveals himself in Scripture, God's word.

Text and context

The historical understanding of the texts and, in this instance, the historical-critical method are very important. The historical-critical approach is often used to such an extent that one fails to appreciate the influence of the Holy Spirit. Texts are interpreted in such a way that their meaning can only be understood in a logical-rational way. The historical-critical method can create specific room to understand the text anew and thus confirm the meaning. This can, however, not be the only method, because rationality can also often be unfounded.

---

23. Alfsvåg, "Postmodern Epistemology," 67.
24. "Belgic Confession."

Barton points out that historical criticism and literary interpretations can relate to each other in a meaningful manner.[25]

The shift to a more structural hermeneutic approach to the texts, with conclusions drawn from the structure, can also facilitate meaningful communication of the classic text.

Thiselton opines that there is considerable room for seeking exegetic freedom.[26] One must, however, guard against hermeneutic anarchy. Although ethics can be an important measure against totally uncertain interpretations, it is not adequate. Manipulation is always a danger.[27] One must take into account the history of the interpretation.[28]

To adapt the text to modern times, the cultural, anthropological, and social background must be taken into account and interpreted in light of what these texts mean in a specific context. Despite the fact that one can agree with Barr that fundamentalism is unfounded, one must also confirm that sound exegesis can include elements whose specific relation can communicate texts directly.[29]

As far as the starting points are concerned, it is clear that crucial questions must be asked as to the way in which the reader and the text meet. The hermeneutical principle is thus very important. In this respect, Van Engen presents clear guidelines by pointing out that the hermeneutical process is not simply a process of unilateral emphasis on aspects.[30] In approaching a text, one will need to address the premises in such a way that the text is not put under stress, resulting in the text not being treated on its merit.

Sound exegesis

What are the principles of sound exegesis? Scripture must be acknowledged for what it wants to be. It is a historical document that still has meaning. Jasper and Boer react to the reformatory approach by emphasizing a hermeneutic of suspicion and regaining the Bible from the left.[31] Although these arguments should be examined in detail, their point of view does

---

25. Barton, "Historical Criticism," 14.
26. Thiselton, "Hermeneutics," 1570.
27. Thiselton, "Hermeneutics," 1571.
28. Thiselton, "Hermeneutics," 1572.
29. Barr, *Bible and Interpretation*, 3–16.
30. Van Engen, *Mission on the Way*, 35–36.
31. Jasper, *Hermeneutics*, 9; Boer, *Rescuing the Bible*, 1–2.

not sufficiently take into account the revelation of God in Scripture. This document about God and man writes meaningfully about the relationship between God and man. Smit emphasizes that the Reformation confirms that Scripture does not have a multitude of meanings (allegorical, typological, spiritual, and moral) but a literal grammatical-historical significance.[32] The Reformers wanted to overcome the abundant interpretations. There is, however, still the challenge to come to a generally acceptable hermeneutic. Scripture reveals the Triune God to man; it is trustworthy and clear about the revelation. The principle of *sacra scriptura sui ipsius interpres est* is still very significant. Although each section of the text must be understood from its own implications, the wider context always helps improve one's insight into the section. Van Engen explains the meaning of narrative theology.[33] Fokkelman emphasizes that, when reading the stories from a narrative point of view, they must be read in accordance with their own rules and conventions.[34] A creative reading is not only linear but also circular, like the latent reading moment.[35] It is not only a "grand narrative"; it is also a hermeneutic starting point that enhances one's understanding of the text. One must read the text critically without dismissing the glorious possibilities that God can do the impossible.

The Holy Spirit renews the reader in such a way that the glory of Christ is made known by what it conveys. This is a living text, not a dead letter. It is alive by him; the emphasis in this instance is initially on the New Testament, due to the specific nature of mission therein. Not only did Jesus himself, in Matthew 28:18–19, give this great instruction, but the book of Acts also explicitly describes the expansion of the church by the preaching of the gospel, to confirm that the Christian message must be conveyed to the world in a unique manner. The apostles, including Paul, conveyed the Christian message, with total dedication, to the people in the world, and this message had specific significance. Paul confronted people with the gospel of Jesus Christ in order to bring them out of darkness into God's wonderful light. This message meant that the renewal brought by the gospel of Jesus Christ touched people's hearts. The gospel of Jesus Christ thus changed their circumstances and way of life. It is crucial to note that

---

32. Smit, *Hermeneutiek*, 12.
33. Van Engen, *Mission on the Way*, 45–52.
34. Fokkelman, *Biblical Narrative*, 19.
35. Fokkelman, *Biblical Narrative*, 21.

the message of the gospel was conveyed in the early church under different circumstances and often despite a great deal of persecution.

The implication of mission bringing people out of darkness into God's wonderful light is still important. Currently, other means are used to approach Voetius's threefold aim of mission, namely *conversio gentilium*, *plantatio ecclesiae*, and *gloria et manifestatio gratiae Divinae* (conversion of the unbelievers, establishment of the church, and the revelation of the honor and glory of God, as quoted in Bosch).[36] Saayman wrote an incisive article on whether the conversion of unbelievers and the last element of Voetius's approach, namely *gloria et manifestatio gratiae Divinae* (the revelation of the honor and glory of God), should be placed on the same level.[37] He dealt with this in light of the two questions raised by *Evangelism Explosion*.[38] First, should you die this evening, are you certain that you will go to heaven? Secondly, why should God allow you into his heaven? Saayman pointed out that the core principle is, in fact, that the honor and glory of God must be sought in mission.[39]

Missio Dei

Bosch in particular came up with interesting principles of mission in his book *Transforming Mission: Paradigm Shifts in Theology of Mission*. In Part 3 of his book, he addresses the rise of the ecumenic mission paradigm. Bosch writes:

> This means that both the centrifugal and centripetal forces in the emerging paradigm—diversity versus unity, divergence versus integration, pluralism versus holism—will have to be taken into account throughout. A crucial notion in this regard will be that of creative tension: it is only within the force field of apparent opposites that we shall begin to approximate a way of theologizing for our own time in a meaningful way.[40]

He points out that this has numerous implications in many disciplines. Mission can not only be viewed as the way in which some people are brought

---

36. Bosch, *Transforming Mission*, 262.
37. Saayman, "Conversion," 159–73.
38. Kennedy, *Evangelism Explosion*.
39. Saayman, "Conversion," 159–73.
40. Bosch, *Transforming Mission*, 367.

to God, but it comprehensively includes many aspects of man's existence. He not only indicates that the church is central,[41] but he also points out the significance of God's kingdom for the church and how the church exists within God's kingdom. The principles of mission must be worked out and understood in many areas of life. Bosch especially emphasizes mission as *missio Dei*.[42] He points out that, in a lecture at the Brandenburg Mission Conference in 1932, Barth emphasized that mission is an activity of God himself. Karel Hartenstein conveyed similar thoughts in 1933. This emphasizes that God is the one who is indeed the Sender. The classic principle in *missio Dei* is that God the Father sends the Son, that God the Father and the Son send the Holy Spirit, and that God the Father, the Son, and the Holy Spirit send the church into the world.[43] Bosch summarizes this strikingly: "Mission has its origin in the heart of God. God is a fountain of sending love. This is the deepest source of mission. It is impossible to penetrate deeper still; there is mission because God loves people."[44]

The principle of *missio Dei* is further developed within the general concept of *missiones ecclesiae*, namely the church's call and task to bring the message of God into the world. Bosch shows that this is not merely about winning souls; rather, God enters this world, initiates the promises of his kingdom, and calls to participation in the battle against the powers of darkness and evil.[45] For this reason, Bosch finds it important to emphasize that mission passes on salvation, but that salvation includes many aspects and is more complete than was understood previously.[46] Mission also includes the search for justice and does not exclude evangelization. Bosch points out that mission is more general than evangelization, but that the latter is central to mission. Evangelization itself is more than simply the verbal preaching of the gospel, for example. Bosch opines that the church's message of mission has entered man's existence as facilitated by Jesus Christ's incarnation.[47] A more colonial view that emphasizes the Western approach of the gospel

---

41. Bosch, *Transforming Mission*, 368.
42. Bosch, *Transforming Mission*, 389.
43. Bosch, *Transforming Mission*, 390.
44. Bosch, *Transforming Mission*, 392.
45. Bosch, *Transforming Mission*, 391.
46. Bosch, *Transforming Mission*, 421.
47. Bosch, *Transforming Mission*, 400.

must shift to a comprehensive approach of reality, especially as far as the lives of individuals in the developing world are concerned.[48]

Skreslet also emphasizes another crucial aspect of mission that flows from the *missio Dei*, namely the shalom or God-given peace.[49] This includes the messianic promises in the Old Testament, as well as the church's task under the present circumstances. The messianic promises must also be understood within their context. In the Old Testament, these promises are directed to the world at the time, but they gain new significance when kept in Christ. Consequently, one must actively seek God's peace. Bevans and Schroeder elaborate on this by referring to six constants in mission, namely: a Christology based on the Spirit; an ecclesiology of service; a realized eschatology; holistic redemption; a positive anthropology; as well as a critical and positive view on culture.[50] Their inclusive, pluralist approach to Christology does not sufficiently take account of Jesus the LORD's uniqueness.

THE MISSIONAL CHURCH

The missional church has become the essential outcome of the *missio Dei*. DeClaissé-Walford explains the nature of the holistic approach of the missional church.[51] In a postmodern world, he determines some premises, namely praise to God, thanksgiving, truth, service to the community from the presence of place and space, priesthood, community responsibility, and hope. According to him, the post-Christianity congregation acts centrifugally and focuses on work in the community through the Holy Spirit. Goheen,[52] Gorman,[53] Guder,[54] and Flemming[55] also elaborate on this. While the biblical text is still treated seriously, there is also a wider understanding of the basis of mission, namely the missional approach to the church and to mission. The missional church is viewed as an expression of mission. The church is, by nature, missional, and that mission is not attached to the

---

48. Bosch, *Transforming Mission*, 421.
49. Skreslet, *Comprehending Mission*, 33.
50. Bevans and Schroeder, *Constants in Context*, 259–304.
51. DeClaissé-Walford, *Mission*, 61–70.
52. Goheen, "Missional Church," 76–77.
53. Gorman, *Becoming the Gospel*, 102.
54. Guder, *Called to Witness*, 40–50.
55. Flemming, *Why Mission?*, xviii–14.

church. The missional church is, however, not viewed as missionary in the traditional sense of the word. For example, Goheen shows that, following on Bosch, the church should be viewed as an alternative community.[56] To him, it is very important that the understanding of mission is the reaching out by Western "Christianity" to others and that there must be new ways of serving the church. Unlike the traditional church of Christianity, the missional church wants to understand the church anew. Goheen understands mission not only as the task of a few individuals, but as the full task of God's people to renew the world as a whole, thus participating in God's story.[57] To him, it is about the salvation of the world as a whole, not only of God's people. They must be a blessing for the world. According to him, the Bible must be read missionally, in order to liberate the church to act in a renewed fashion.[58] Gorman indicates that Paul's message about mission includes justice for the world as a whole.[59] Justice is thus not only a spiritual renewal but also includes the essential task that justice be done. According to him, it reduces the message of salvation if it does not include the total justice of all people and creation as a whole. Guder also dismisses the idea of "Christianity" and points to the great division in Western Christianity that is conveyed to the world, where mission took place.[60] The *missio Dei* is the way in which the mystery, freedom, and pluralism of the gospel must be conveyed, according to him. Flemming, who wants to treat Scripture seriously, points out that mission must also be understood widely to include total salvation for creation.[61]

Niemandt addresses the issue as to how missiology must be considered in light of the World Council of Churches' document entitled *Together towards Life: Mission and Evangelism in Changing Landscapes* and mentions that missiology must take this seriously.[62] Niemandt mentions that the new approach should consider Christian mission anew, based on the Triune God, to also convey and confirm the full kingdom of God.[63] Niemandt concludes by mentioning that the theology in this document wants to reach the poor

56. Goheen, "Missional Church," 482–83.
57. Goheen, Missional Reading of the Bible," 21–27.
58. Goheen, "Missional Reading of the Bible," 27.
59. Gorman, *Becoming the Gospel*, 257.
60. Guder, *Called to Witness*, 40–45.
61. Flemming, *Why Mission?*, xviii–14.
62. Niemandt, "Towards New Life for Missiology," 82–103.
63. Niemandt, "Towards New Life for Missiology," 83.

and the marginalized and break down the walls that divide, dehumanize, discriminate, reject, and exclude.[64] Lesslie Newbigin emphasizes this idea of the church in his book entitled *The Gospel in a Pluralist Society*.[65] On his return to Great Britain, Newbigin, who served as missionary in India, found many challenges for mission in society. In India, membership of the church and renewal of the church were essential aspects in one's life. In Western society, where the Christian gospel is accepted as a matter of course, the gospel does not totally renew people's lives. Newbigin then raised the question: How can the church in such a situation exist as a missional church, as a church that lives from the renewal?[66] How can that renewal bring about significant change? This would imply that Newbigin viewed the church's renewal from this total change and significant existence in society.[67]

Another issue that needs to be emphasized and that Van Engen especially raised in *God's Missionary People: Rethinking the Purpose of the Local Church* is that the different aspects of the life of the church, namely *kerugma*, *koinonia*, *diakonia*, and *marturia*, establish the church as God's mission people.[68] This has significance for the church's existence in the world. On the basis of *kerugma*, the church must preach the word and bring salvation to people. On the basis of *diakonia*, the church must also render a service to show the world as a whole that service and care of people occurs in the church. On the basis of the *marturia*, the church must witness the salvation in Christ. On the basis of the *koinonia*, the church must form society to love and care for each other so that they can reach out to one another. The church must thus be the society where people come together. As far as *leiturgia* is concerned, the church brings total renewal in Christ. This renewal of mission includes all aspects of society, touches every aspect of life, and renews every aspect of society.

Of course, the traditional concept of the church of Christianity must be criticized. There are a number of beautiful aspects in missional movement as well as differences in specific elements of mission. At most, mission is preaching, in word and deed, that Jesus Christ is the only LORD who wants to lead people in the deepest darkness of sin, through the Holy Spirit,

---

64. Niemandt, "Towards New Life for Missiology," 99.

65. Newbigin, *Gospel in a Pluralist Society*, 8–12.

66. Newbigin, *Gospel in a Pluralist Society*, 8–12.

67. See also Pillay, "Missional Renaissance," 6; Nel, "Dwelling in the Word," 6; Niemandt, "Acts for Today's Missional Church," 1–6; Mukawa, "Transformation," 245.

68. Van Engen, *God's Missionary People*, 41–45.

in praise of the Father of love, to new and eternal life. It is abundantly clear in both 2 Corinthians 5:1–10[69] and John 14:1–14 that heavenly glory awaits the faithful after death and that this must be preached to the entire world. It is also true that it is dreadful to fall into the hands of the living God if you are not in Christ (Heb 10:31). This is, however, the significance of Jesus Christ's death on the cross. He wants to effect radical redemption through the Holy Spirit. There is hope for all. This premise is better expressed by the concept of "missionary."

BASIS OF MISSION

Bavinck emphasizes that mission finds its basis in God's incredibly merciful turn towards man in Jesus Christ.[70] According to him, this is the only basis. Van Engen defines mission clearly as the deliberate crossing of borders by God's people; from church to no church and from belief to disbelief, to proclaim the great wonder of the coming of God's kingdom in Jesus Christ, in word and deed.[71] To Van Engen, redemption is a specific element of mission through the church's participation in God's mission. That redemption includes redemption with God, the people themselves, their fellow human beings, and the world. People congregate in the church through conversion and belief in Jesus Christ, through the Holy Spirit, thus renewing the world. The church is also a sign of the coming of the kingdom of God in Jesus Christ.

God brings redemption in Christ in a unique way. On the other hand, one must also understand that God's shift to the world does not include universalism. God's salvation also calls for conversion and change, and the Holy Spirit works on rebirth and conversion. This does not mean that there will be universal change and that all people will be saved. In this regard, one can refer to John 6:37: "All those the Father gives me will come to me, and whoever comes to me I will never drive away."

The tension between those who believe and those who do not believe is very clear in this instance. In John 6, some Jews stated: "How can he now say, 'I am the bread that came down from heaven?'" Jesus answers in John 6:53–58: "Very truly I tell you, unless you eat the flesh of the Son of Man

---

69. See Verster, "Abode in Heaven," 19–33.
70. Bavinck, *Science of Mission*, 62.
71. Van Engen, *Mission on the Way*, 26–27.

and drink his blood, you have no life in you. Whoever eats my flesh and drinks my blood has eternal life, and I will raise them up at the last day."

Jesus also clearly states that whoever sins is a slave of sin.

John 8:34 elaborates on this: "Everyone who sins is a slave to sin. Now a slave has no permanent place in the family, but a son belongs to it forever. So, if the Son sets you free, you will be free indeed."

Jesus concludes by saying that Abraham rejoiced at the thought of seeing his day. Then Jesus told them specifically that belief in him is the way in which salvation will be realized. With regard to this salvation, one can thus sin, thus totally rejecting Christ and opposing the conviction of the Holy Spirit so persistently that Christ's work is ultimately not acknowledged. This will eventually mean that Christ's glory is not acknowledged significantly. Jesus must be worshipped at all times. The spirit of the times may never be defining.

Wright defines mission as follows: "Fundamentally, our mission (if it is biblically informed and validated) means our committed participation as God's people, at God's invitation and command, in God's own mission within the history of God's world for the redemption of God's creation."[72]

Mission is thus holistic and comprehensive. There will, however, always be a spearhead in respect of evangelization and conveying the glorious message to people so that they can be brought from the darkness into God's wonderful light. In his comprehensive work *Early Christian Mission* on early mission, Schnabel points out how mission will bring the good news of Jesus Christ to the world.[73] Schnabel confirms the way in which mission works:

> The New Testament documents portray the apostles as messengers who proclaim the good news of Jesus Christ, heal the sick and help the members of the new communities of believers in Jesus to grow and support each other in love, faith and hope, as they implement Jesus' example and commission to preach the gospel and heal the sick (Matt 10:7–8), make all nations into disciples (Matt 28:19–20) and witness to his life, death and resurrection unto the ends of the earth (Acts 1:3, 8). The goal of the universal and international mission to the nations—Jews and Gentiles alike—was to be reached "by word and deed."[74]

---

72. Wright, *Mission of God*, 22.
73. Schnabel, *Early Christian Mission*.
74. Schnabel, *Early Christian Mission*, 2.1548.

Apostles and missionaries of the church were prepared to proclaim that Jesus is the true Messiah.[75]

Is everything then mission? Walter Freitag's warning still applies: If everything becomes mission, then nothing is mission.[76] Mission is always defined by the principle of mission in the world, namely that the wonderful gospel of Jesus brings people from darkness into God's wonderful light. Pocock, Van Rheenen, and McConnell address the challenges of mission. In the body of Christ lies the challenge to convey the message of salvation to the world:

> Mutual respect and appreciation, sincere love, and a desire to benefit from what we have all learned about the LORD in each of our cultures should characterize Christians.[77]

To understand this clearly, incisive remarks must be made on sin. The severity of the sin must be pointed out. There must be no doubt that sin infiltrated humanity totally. Sin permeates man's entire existence. It affects every aspect of humanness and of man's life. It is a total break from God. Only when the severity of sin is understood can one react thereto and realize that Jesus Christ's death on the cross is the only answer for this.[78] For this reason, Paul calls for new life.

Mission is the ministry of God's reconciliation. The entire salvation of redemption from sin is found only in Jesus Christ. Mission is thus always the recognition of the total transcendence of God who brought salvation for the whole of creation in this world through the church.

A broad understanding of mission is indeed essential, but one will also have to guard against the idea that mission can be understood only within the missional church. The full significance of mission, which also means that from the wonder of Christ there is an approach in Christology within Trinitarian theology to bring people from darkness into God's wonderful light, must still be taken into account. There is the danger in the missional church where mission simply evaporates, as a disposition among people, and that this disposition among people must determine mission. From a scriptural perspective, mission as such has a strong sense of proclaiming the gospel, a call to conversion and radical turn to God that must be

---

75. Schnabel, *Early Christian Mission*, 1.551.
76. Freitag, *Reden und Aufsätze*, 11.94.
77. Pocock et al., *Changing Face of World Missions*, 156–57.
78. See Verster, *Christian Mission*, 14.

emphasized on the basis of the proclamation of the word. Mission always emphasizes the radical significance of the free grace of God. Transcendence is not negotiable. Mission must be approached from Christ. Salvation in Christ is comprehensive and includes a total approach to what is important for the different aspects of life.

Kritzinger (J. N. J.), however, follows an approach in mission where attention is paid to a meeting between various religious convictions and religions.[79] He calls this "encounterology." In this regard, he refers to ways in which such a meeting can take place. Kritzinger understands that attention must be paid to specific issues:

1. Agency: Who you are.
2. Context analysis: What are the social, political, economic, and cultural factors that determine the meeting?
3. Ecclesial analysis: What was and is the behavior of Christian communities of faith towards others?
4. Theological reflection: How is the Bible interpreted in light of the above?
5. Spirituality: Which spirituality is followed?
6. Practical projects: Which projects are tackled in relation to other religious convictions?
7. Reflexivity: How are all the above continuously integrated?[80]

From a theological point of view, one can not agree with Kritzinger on everything. Many aspects of Kritzinger's views are important and should be regarded as such, but one may not ignore the essence of the confession that Jesus is the only LORD. This must still be confessed with humility, love, and subservience. Others will never be approached with pride, self-importance, or self-justification. This will only be acknowledged in total dependency on God.

How is mission understood in this present book?

Mission is the action of the Triune God, the Father, the Son, and the Holy Spirit who brings salvation and redemption in Jesus Christ for people and for the world. Mission proclaims that Jesus is the true LORD and that he as LORD must be acknowledged. He leads people, through the Holy

---

79. Kritzinger, "Encounterology," 764.
80. Kritzinger, "Encounterology," 771–72.

Spirit, from darkness into God's wonderful light, so that they experience in this life the fullness of life but also inherit eternal life because they are more than victorious in Jesus Christ. Mission is life from this confession so that the church, through the Holy Spirit, serves, helps, and blesses with love in the expectation of eternity.

Jesus, Son of God, Is Our Atonement

Missionary Christology approaches Christology from the perspective of the revelation and significance of Jesus Christ for the world. This is already a specific starting point, but it is only the beginning. The person and work of Christ are central. Christology determines the theology concerning the approach to the current crises in the world. Who is Jesus Christ? What must be believed about him? What is the meaning of Jesus Christ with respect to man in crisis? What is the significance of his behavior on earth for man in all his/her aspects? How does Christ's deed of reconciliation affect man's future in the world? What is the significance of Jesus Christ for eternity and eternal life? Is there an acceptable Christological point of view that provides clear guidelines as to the church's confession about him and as such confirms the church's presence in the world? Does this mean that Christology must be a Christology from "below"? Or does Christ himself determine Christology and who he is and what he is, such as in the confession of Nicaea and the decisions of Chalcedon, definitely expressed in this respect? Not only is it confessed that he is "God from God, Light from Light, true God from true God,"[1] but also that he is fully human and that his two natures are combined in a wonderful way: *asungutos, atreptos, adiaretos, achoristos* (pure, immutable, one, not separate). How does one understand this confession, and what is its significance for the world? Is it still a relevant confession? Is this not already a choice for a Christology derived from Western philosophical thought? The question is: What is the origin of the Christian belief regarding Jesus? Based on this belief, one must talk with others. Incisive answers must be sought in terms of various challenges facing current Christology.

1. "Nicene Creed."

THE HISTORICAL JESUS

To determine who Jesus Christ really is, one must also inquire about the significance of his preexistence and his earthly life. Missionary Christology will thus judge all the different aspects regarding the sovereignty of Christ before attempting to provide clear guidelines to understand Christ for mission. The starting point that he is our atonement will still have to be considered. Of course, this is linked to the insightful confession regarding Christ as Son of God who became fully human. One must then also judge this confession and determine its significance from specific premises. This is crucial for considering the significance of Jesus Christ for mission. As opinions often differ, one will have to react to the points of view of various exponents. The emphasis is on Christ's three functions, namely king, priest, and prophet. This is not only deduced from specific titles, but from the specific meaning of those functions in both the Old and the New Testament. Jesus lends a totally new meaning to this. This will be explained in detail later.

There is often doubt about Jesus' divinity. It is alleged that Jesus did good to other people, and this is the way religion must be practiced. It is thought that he was the good human being *par excellence* and that the good which he did must be emphasized, not his two natures (Chalcedon). It is, however, clear that this is a serious attenuation of the gospel.

Welker raises the question: Who is Jesus Christ for us nowadays?[2] He refers to important aspects, which Bonhoeffer already mentioned, namely that only the suffering God can help and that the presence of Jesus Christ in the suffering is very important. Bonhoeffer's first contribution is that only the suffering God can help. The second contribution is that God bears us in the multicontextuality of life. Welker adds a so-called fourth quest.[3] Welker writes:

> The fourth level of multicontextuality, the level facilitating the "fourth quest for the historical Jesus," involves the entire previous history of reception along with the present global multicontextuality within which Jesus' life and ministry are being actively received, on the one hand, and are in their own turn efficaciously active, on the other.[4]

---

2. Welker, *God the Revealed: Christology*, 11–15.
3. Welker, *God the Revealed: Christology*, 87–90.
4. Welker, *God the Revealed: Christology*, 90.

He opines that multicontextuality guides this quest. It must be acknowledged that archaeological reports have a historical authenticity, but that the various reports do confirm that Jesus' significance can be found in multicontextuality.

Welker emphasizes the multicontextuality of the approach to Jesus Christ who conveys various aspects of his glory in a multicontextual reality; this multicontextuality leads to a deeper understanding of his sovereignty. This highlights Jesus' specific significance.[5] According to Welker, the fourth quest attempts not only to judge contemporary issues such as desires, moral dilemmas, religious needs, and directions, as well as that which applies wrongly to Jesus, nor to consider the difference in the present modalities and conjuncture of Jesus' time but also analyzes Jesus' present, past, and future, as mentioned in various reports on him. As it has now become impossible to write about Jesus, Welker opines that the multicontextual complexity of the new quest moves from an impossible problem to a promising investigation.[6] This multicontextual investigation enables one to guard against the reasoning of, for example, Crossan[7] or Vermes.[8]

It is extremely important that the historical Jesus and the Jesus of faith both established that he comes from God. In one's approach to the historical Jesus, one must not premise that Jesus is simply human and does not come from God. In considering the various aspects of the historical Jesus, one must indicate the clear characteristics of Jesus as the one who comes from God. The historical Jesus would be ignored if one does not acknowledge that he comes from God. It is indeed so that, from a positivist perspective, the historical Jesus is indeed simply a human being, and one must accept his humanness and positive disposition. However, this is not possible. One must understand that Scripture also mentions that the historical Jesus is the one who comes from God, as the one who is from God, and as the one who is one with God. This means that the evidence regarding the historical Jesus must also take into account that Jesus Christ is truly God who has come to us. In this instance, one must also consider Jesus' preexistence.

---

5. Welker, *God the Revealed: Christology*, 90.
6. Welker, *God the Revealed: Christology*, 92.
7. Crossan, *Historical Jesus*, 395–425.
8. Vermes, *Changing Faces of Jesus*, 220–30.

THE PREEXISTENCE OF JESUS CHRIST WHO IS OUR ATONEMENT

One must now accurately explore the significance of Jesus' preexistence and the witness that he is the Son of God and truly God. This has specific meaning for the atonement he effects. One must consider and compare the various opinions on this. Scripture will be considered once the differences and similarities in the opinions have been pointed out. Jesus Christ is unique, not because he emphasizes love for one's neighbor or because of his miracles. Jesus Christ's preexistence distinguishes him from all other religious leaders.

Exponents on Jesus Christ's divinity

Calvin: Jesus Christ as true God and true human being

Calvin leaves no doubt that Jesus Christ is miraculously one with God.[9] From the beginning, God is revealed as three persons in one being, as the true God. The Father, the Son, and the Spirit is one God; yet the Son is not the Father, and the Spirit is not the Son.[10] Christ's divinity and eternity are one.[11] Christ's miracles are further proof of his deity.[12] He is also invoked in prayer—something that only belongs to God. Calvin also emphasizes that the distinction in three persons does not revoke the unity of God, because the Son is One with God the Father; together they have one Spirit, and the Spirit is the Spirit of the Father and of the Son.[13] Calvin never denies Christ's human nature, but simply emphasizes that the Father, the Son, and the Spirit are One and that Jesus Christ's divinity is beyond any doubt.[14]

---

9. Calvin, *Institusie*, 1.iii.1–2.
10. Calvin, *Institusie*, 1. iii.5.
11. Calvin, *Institusie*, 1.iii.8.
12. Calvin, *Institusie*, 1.iii.13.
13. Calvin, *Institusie*, 1.iii.19.
14. Calvin, *Institusie*, 11.xii.1.

Barth: Jesus Christ as the true revelation of the Totally Different

One must incisively discuss the issue of the divinity of Christ, especially in respect of the theology of Barth.[15] God is viewed as the Totally Different, as the one who, in his sovereignty and majesty, is totally different to human life.[16] The divinity of Christ is again strongly emphasized. Should one then understand that Christ is the one who comes from God, the Word of God, and that he must be viewed as one with God? Barth's theology is interesting in this instance. Barth shows that the unity of God and Christ is, in a special way, a link between the sovereignty of the heavenly God and the earthly individual.[17] Barth writes:

> Between God and man there stands the person of Jesus Christ, Himself God and Himself man, and so mediating between the two. In Him God reveals Himself to man. In Him man sees and knows God. In Him God stands before man and man stands before God, as is the eternal will of God, and the eternal ordination of man in accordance with this will. In Him God's plan for man is disclosed, God's judgement on man fulfilled, God's deliverance of man accomplished, God's gift to man present in fulness, God's claim and promise to man declared. In Him, God has joined Himself to man.[18]

Barth views Jesus Christ as the only Word of God. If Jesus must be honored in this world, he must always be honored on the basis of the concept that he is the only Word of God (John 1:1). Although one can differ with the formulation the emphasis on the sovereignty of Christ is especially significant. For Barth, the significance of Jesus lies in the fact that he came to bring salvation. The true Word of God is Jesus Christ, and one can not discuss Jesus without acknowledging that he truly comes from God, thus enabling one to emphasize the sovereignty of Jesus Christ in a very unique and specific way.

---

15. Barth, *Church Dogmatics* 2/1:94–95, 2/2:94–95.
16. Barth, *Church Dogmatics* 2/1:273.
17. Barth, *Church Dogmatics* 2/2:94–95.
18. Barth, *Church Dogmatics* 2/2:94–95

Kärkkäinen: The preexistence of Jesus

Kärkkäinen indicates that Christology includes the first principles of the Chalcedonian definition.[19] Kärkkäinen explains the significance of Chalcedon as follows:

> In the final analysis, the question of the continuing value of the Chalcedonian formula is a wide-ranging hermeneutical decision. A related question is the genre of the Definition itself. Its basic affirmation, namely, the coming together of the divine and human in an irreversible yet distinguishable unity, can be appropriately called a mystery and metaphor. It is mystery in the sense that it goes beyond human capacity to understand. It is paradox in the sense that it is a statement against our expectations. However, it is not paradox in the sense of being so much against reason that it is a contradictory or senseless statement. Finally, it is metaphor in the sense defined above: a picture of reality that goes beyond ordinary language, yet depicts events that have happened. So, it is a "true" metaphor.[20]

Kärkkäinen leaves no doubt that one must accept a metaphysical recognition of Jesus Christ's incarnation.[21]

Dunn: Progression concerning the confession of Jesus' preexistence

The issue of preexistence is thus extremely important. Dunn queries the acknowledgment of Christ's preexistence in the earliest sources.[22] He opines that the development of the confession concerning preexistence derives from the religious conviction and opinions of the Hellenistic context of early Christians. For that reason, they established the preexistence of Jesus, which was viewed as something that developed within the theological thought of early Christians.

Dunn opines that there is a definite progression in understanding Christology in the New Testament.[23] The incarnation of Christ as Son of

---

19. Kärkkäinen, *Christ and Reconciliation*, 114.
20. Kärkkäinen, *Christ and Reconciliation*, 114.
21. Kärkkäinen, *Christ and Reconciliation*, 116
22. Dunn, *Christology*, 114.
23. Dunn, *Christology*, 262.

God does not mean, for example, that Christ himself has a clear image of an understanding of his eternal life with God and his incarnation.

Dunn's contribution is important, but one can point out a number of gaps. Already in Philippians 2, Paul emphasizes Jesus' total unity with God. This is the early witness of unity with God. Colossians 1 also clearly confirms that the unity with God is not negotiable. I will refer to this in more detail later.

On the other hand, Dunn acknowledges that Jesus was professed as God from God later in the church, but he does not mention that this already occurs in the earliest New Testament sources. Dunn points out that one must highlight a progression, a development in thought concerning the salvation of God. In discussion with Dunn, it can and will be pointed out how the earliest sources already acknowledged Jesus Christ as Son of God, as God from God.

Schreiner: Jesus as true Son of God

Unlike Dunn, Schreiner finds a link between what Paul understands about Christ and the kingdom of the House of David, the messianic kingdom.[24] He understands that Christ was viewed as a unique revelation of God from the new kingdom that originated from David, and the Adam Christology and the Abrahamic meaning of Christ as descendant of Abraham. He opines that Paul mentions Jesus' specific relationship with God when he uses the concept of "Son of God." Israel and David are called to act as new Adam and sons of God, but Israel and David failed. The true Adam and the true Son of God are emphasized only in Jesus. Therefore, Adam's true sovereignty was awarded to him. This is reflected in the fact that he rose from death. Schreiner also emphasizes that the fundamental topic in Scripture is that YHWH is both God and LORD.[25] Those who humiliate themselves before God as the LORD and acknowledge him also acknowledge that the Son, Christ, must be acknowledged as LORD.

Schreiner's understanding of Philippians 2:6–11 is that exceptional significance is given to Christ as the one who is in a unique relationship with God. He does emphasize the Adam Christology, but he differs from Dunn's interpretation.

---

24. Schreiner, *King in His Beauty*, 544–46.
25. Schreiner, *King in His Beauty*, 547.

From a more classical approach, Schreiner acknowledges that Jesus Christ must be acknowledged as God from God. In that respect, he differs from Dunn and points out that, from Scripture as a whole, the confession about Jesus is of special significance. He, therefore, confirms that Jesus Christ has unique significance. In his answer to Dunn, Schreiner points out that full salvation is in Christ as Redeemer.

Hurtado: Jesus Christ as the One who is worshipped

Hurtado explores early Christianity in detail and raises the question as to how those early communities acknowledged Jesus Christ as God who became human.[26] From the outset, Hurtado highlights the acknowledgment and worshipping of Christ as an important issue. Hurtado emphasizes that worshipping Jesus occurs early on: "At an astonishing early point, in at least some Christian groups, there is a clear and programmatic inclusion of Jesus in their devotional life, both in honorific claims and in devotional practices."[27]

It is important to note that Hurtado does not pass judgment on the worshipping of Jesus. He confirms that the worship of Jesus in the early communities means that specific significance was attached to Christ, and that Christ must thus be understood as the unique person who comes from God. According to Hurtado, Jesus' inclusion in the worshipping by early Christian groups was an indication, at this very early stage, that Jesus must be worshipped as a special person.[28]

Hurtado shows that the Jews acknowledged God as the only God.[29] The thought among early Christian circles that Jesus, in a very unique way, is an agent of God the Father and that he must be worshipped in the same way as God did not occur among the Jews. Hurtado summarizes his point of view as follows:

> The early convictions about Jesus and the corresponding devotion offered to him that became so widespread in earliest Christianity were sufficiently robust to nourish the prolonged and

---

26. Hurtado, *Jesus Christ*, 4.
27. Hurtado, *Jesus Christ*, 4.
28. Hurtado, *Jesus Christ*, 4.
29. Hurtado, *Jesus Christ*, 31.

vigorous efforts to articulate Christian faith in persuasive doctrinal formulations.[30]

Hurtado very strongly shows that the worshipping of Jesus already occurred in the earliest forms of the early church. He explicitly mentions that this worshipping was associated with the worshipping of YHWH. It would be unthinkable for Jews to worship another person than YHWH, but Jesus was worshipped in a similar fashion as YHWH. Hurtado expressly shows that the early church emphasized that the worshipping of Jesus was on the same level as that of YHWH. In the earliest witnesses of the early church, Jesus Christ was already acknowledged as the one who must be worshipped in the same way as the Only God in the Jewish faith.

Wright: Jesus Christ and the confession of monotheism

In his interesting book on Paul, *Paul and the Faithfulness of God*, N. T. Wright highlights several issues that are of interest to Christology.[31] Initially, Wright points out that Paul must be understood in his own world from his relationship to, among others, the wisdom of Athens, the religious and cultural worlds, and Roman society.[32] He emphasizes especially that, if one wants to understand Paul, one must fully understand his theology from the relationship with the Jewish faith.[33] Wright indicates that Paul's most profound conviction is that Jesus Christ is the full revelation of the one true God who is known as the true Messiah.[34] Wright makes a strong statement:

> As Messiah, Jesus was the one in whom God's faithfulness had come to climatic expression, and who therefore called out faithfulness from his followers. Here is a point of great symbolic significance before it can be explored as a central point of theology: loyalty to Jesus as Messiah, "the obedience of faith" as Paul puts it, occupies the place within Paul's new worldview-construct formerly occupied by the "loyalty to God," or to the Torah, or to the Holy Land, within just that zealous Judaism that we know to have been Paul's own context.[35]

30. Hurtado, *Jesus Christ*, 650.
31. Wright, *Paul, Parts III and IV*, 197–200
32. Wright, *Paul, Parts III and IV*, 197–200.
33. Wright, *Paul, Parts III and IV*, 140–45.
34. Wright, *Paul, Parts III and IV*, 644–45.
35. Wright, *Paul, Parts III and IV*, 405.

For this reason, he reveals himself as the one true God of Israel. Paul finds that he reveals himself again in Jesus Christ.[36] One can definitely agree with Wright: Paul very strongly emphasizes the centrality of monotheism. Jesus Christ is not viewed as a second God besides God. Jesus is understood with relation to monotheism, and this must be strongly emphasized.

Wright strongly stresses the significance of Jesus Christ in light of the monotheist acknowledgment in the Jewish faith. Although Wright explores different aspects, his emphasis on Jesus Christ as the true Son of God, in the context of monotheism, is of great interest. This is the reason why he places so much emphasis on Jesus as the true Messiah who brings salvation and redemption to people in his life. Jesus replaces Israel. Despite the criticism against Wright's thought, one must stress that Jesus as true Messiah takes the entire role of Israel upon himself. Within the context of Jewish monotheism, he must be acknowledged as the one who is from God.

Van de Beek: God is One

Van de Beek mentions that this broken, destructive world does not have the last word.[37] The last word belongs to the Messiah King, the Crucified. In this world, Christ is the Crucified; in this world, we follow him as followers of the Crucified, and we must follow the Crucified as broken humans, because he is a broken man in this world. One must thus agree with Van de Beek that Christ the Crucified was driven from this world and that the circle around the Messiah is the circle of suffering.[38]

Van de Beek views the fall of humans into sin as radical and complete.[39] He emphasizes that Christ became a full human being in order to share the misery of humans. God shares (participates) in the brokenness and misery of humans. The holy God identifies with humans. God himself is present in Jesus Christ the LORD in humans' need, anxiety, and sorrow.

Van de Beek does not accept a potential development towards a better future, but he does point out that God in Jesus Christ brings salvation for humans in that humans can also share in God-given salvation. Reconciliation occurs when humans participate in the suffering and resurrection

---

36. Wright, *Paul, Parts III and IV*, 118.
37. Van de Beek, A. *Jezus Kurios*, 26.
38. Van de Beek, A. *Kring om de Messias*, 54.
39. Van de Beek, A. *Jezus Kurios*, 25.

of Jesus. Jesus Christ is one with God, and because God is One, there is salvation.

Van de Beek points out that the texts which refer to Christ's subjection and obedience stress his divinity because that subjection and obedience is from God, due to his presence.[40] This shows that he comes from God because he is the true God who is present and is obedient in this world. There is no other God, and there is no other salvation to be obtained without the will of God and without the representation of Jesus as the one who acquires justice from God for us.

Of interest is the special meaning Van de Beek attaches to the fact that God is One. He emphasizes that God is One, and because he is One, one must acknowledge that Jesus Christ is One in that relationship with God. Van de Beek strongly opts for full transcendence in Christology. One must also acknowledge this, as it is very important. This, as it were, concludes the thought that one must move away from Christ's limitation once one acknowledges his full transcendence. Van de Beek creates room for us to understand how great the glory of Christ is in his unity with God. This is of specific significance for understanding Christology.

SUMMARY

Of great importance are the irrefutable proofs by Wright and Hurtado that one must understand the evidence concerning Jesus Christ in the Gospels and in Paul, in light of Jewish monotheism. Although there were, among Jews, some references to figures such as angels and prophets (Moses) who were specifically exalted, they were never understood in light of the monotheistic God. It is different with Jesus. He is understood as one with the monotheistic God, despite theologians who essentially underplay this in the New Testament. These convictions must also be tested now in light of exegetic and hermeneutic considerations.

There are a number of exponents on the concept of Jesus Christ in Christology. Many of these exponents emphasize the unity of Father and Son. This glory directs us to the transcendence of Christ and the Father. This implies that one must very strongly emphasize that Christ and the Father are one, and that, in theological reflection, one must grapple with the question: What is the full significance of Christ for mission? This implies incisive thought and approaching the exponents. Calvin emphasizes the

---

40. Van de Beek, A. *Jezus Kurios*, 120.

salvation of God in Christ, the Son of God. Barth emphasizes Jesus Christ as the Only Word of God. Kärkkäinen emphasizes that Jesus Christ must, in this unique sense within the historical context, be understood as from God. Dunn, with whom his concept of Christ's preexistence was discussed, develops new thoughts within this specific context that must be judged. N. T. Wright, with his strong emphasis on the Messiah Christ as true Israel, highlights monotheism. Hurtado undeniably proves that both Christ and YHWH were worshipped in the early church.

Van de Beek emphasizes the wonderful salvation in Christ who is transcendently one with God. That salvation creates the significant acknowledgment of Jesus as LORD.

Exegetic and Hermeneutic Considerations Regarding the Glory of Jesus Christ as Our Redeemer

INTRODUCTION

IN AN APPROACH TO SCRIPTURE, one must endeavor, from the unity of the Scriptures, to convey the witness about God. This means that both the Old and the New Testament must be taken into account. To do so, one must raise the question as to the significance of the eternity of God. It is, therefore, important to consider the witness about God in the Old Testament.

It is specifically significant to understand Christ when a parallel is drawn between the eternity of YHWH in the Old Testament and the eternity of Christ in the New Testament. This is emphasized in several ways. Christ is awarded the title of *Kurios*. Christ is awarded the honorary title of LORD that belongs solely to YHWH. Christ is the Son of God who is God from eternity to eternity. The Gospel of John, in particular, acknowledges the eternity of God and that Christ must also be understood on the basis of YHWH's eternity. God reveals himself as the Eternal. Jesus is revealed as the Son of God. John points out that he reveals himself as the one who is what he is. As such, his glory is uniquely bound to the eternity of YHWH and his confirmation of glory in the Old Testament. A line runs within the context of the covenant of God, who reveals himself as the Eternal One and Totally Different to humans, that also occurs in Christ. He who is revealed as the wonderful is the LORD who, in his glory, creates the possibility of new relationships. The Old Testament is linked with the New Testament, thus confirming Christ's glory.

It is important to listen to the various voices that emphasize the eternity of both God and Christ. Even if some of these voices come from divergent points of view, they confirm the same issue. One must also do exegetic research. Besides discussing specific texts, the language aspect applies to certain key texts that enable one to draw informative conclusions.

PERSPECTIVES IN THE NEW TESTAMENT

The New Testament does not have an abstract, worked-out concept of "eternity." Life in eternity is associated with God's Son (John 6:51, 58). The world and humans have a beginning and an end. God, however, remains the same (Ps 102:28; in Heb 1:12 applied to Christ). Christ is the unchangeable (John 1:1–2; Col 1:15–20; Rev 1:4, 8).

Collett shows that, throughout the centuries, there were different opinions on the relationship between Christ and the Old Testament, and that various sources point to tension in understanding Christ and the world of the Old Testament.[1] He points out that, since Marcion, people have opined that the Old Testament can not be read from a Christocentric point of view, and that there is a radical difference between the Old Testament and the New Testament. He, however, wants to read the Old Testament book of Psalms from a Christomorphic perspective and asks whether the Old Testament book of Psalms mentions Christ in reality. He refers to Psalms 1 and 2, which indicate that the anointed of the LORD can apply to Christ.

Goldingay emphasizes that Jesus announces the kingdom of God.[2] This, in turn, emphasizes that Jesus is the one who reveals God and comes from God. God is addressed as Father,[3] and this stresses that Jesus is the one who proclaims the kingdom. For this reason, he is truly the one who proclaims redemption and glory. He himself is anointed as King[4] and as the Son of God.[5] His divine behavior is very clear in what he does, and one can, therefore, acknowledge that Jesus, in light of the Old Testament emphasis on the uniqueness of YHWH, is the unique Son of God.[6]

1. Collett, "Christology," 390–95.
2. Goldingay, *Israel's Gospel*, 709.
3. Goldingay, *Israel's Gospel*, 794.
4. Goldingay, *Israel's Gospel*, 814.
5. Goldingay, *Israel's Gospel*, 823.
6. Goldingay, *Israel's Gospel*, 840.

EXEGETIC AND HERMENEUTIC CONSIDERATIONS

This issue is of great interest. When one understands Christ within this context of the eternity of God and the self-revelation of God, it is clear that one must also mention Christ who introduces himself to humans and that his revelation, as indicated in the Gospels, clearly shows one who he is. The question must thus be raised as to whether Jesus himself already viewed himself as Son of God, and whether, in his revelation, he made it clear that he is the Son of God. There are different opinions on this topic. Christ himself did not view himself as Messiah, Redeemer, and LORD, but he acted within the circumstances of the day and, according to Schweitzer, he dies as a disenchanted man because the kingdom of God, which he proclaimed, has not dawned as he expected.[7]

On the contrary, one must examine the New Testament exegetically and hermeneutically. One must consider Jesus Christ's glory as Son of God.

The glory of Christ in Matthew

In Matthew, the glory of Jesus Christ is emphasized in a very unique way in that he is portrayed as the one who comes from the generation of David and Immanuel, "God with us." The name Immanuel, "God with us," also emphasizes the glory of Christ as the one who comes from God. Other sections in Matthew, in which the glory of Christ is introduced, elaborate on this. John the Baptist (Matt 3:11–12) refers to Jesus' exceptional glory.

The glory and majesty of Jesus are stated very clearly in this instance. The Sermon on the Mount is also mentioned when he does what only God can do, and when he says, "But I tell them." God alone can say that he gives them the new law and the new implications of the law. When Jesus gives them the implications of the new law and conveys the new significance of the various aspects thereof in the Sermon on the Mount, it is obvious that Jesus is the one whose uniqueness is emphasized. His miracles, his glory, his rising from the dead, and his healings highlight Jesus' glory. Jesus' invitation in Matthew (11:25–30) highlights this.

Turner states this very clearly:

> 11:27 Jesus turns from prayer to affirmation of his unique messianic status as the exclusive revelator of the Father. The Father has delegated all things to the Son (cf. 28:18), with whom he shares a unique relationship of intimate reciprocal knowledge. This is not unlike the relationship of God and wisdom in Hellenistic Jewish

---

7. Schweitzer, *Historical Jesus*, 386–90.

texts that reflect on Proverbs 1:20–23; 8:1–36 (e.g., Sir 1:6–9; 24:19–22; 51:23–30; Bar 3:32; Wis 8:4; 9:1–18; 10:10). Here the trinitarian basis of Jesus's messianic mission, previously seen at Jesus's baptism, is reiterated and developed (cf. Matt. 3:17; 12:18; 17:5; 28:18–19). The unique relationship of the Father and the Son in redeeming God's people is clearly described in 11:25–27.[8]

Mark

In Mark 1:1, Jesus Christ is described as the Son of God. The phrase "Son of God" does not occur in all the manuscripts. Mark's Gospel strongly emphasizes the line that runs throughout, namely that Jesus Christ is the one who brings redemption and the kingdom of God closer.

The prophetic discourse in Mark further emphasizes what glory awaits he who acknowledges that Jesus is the Christ. His majesty and glory are confirmed. At the institution of the LORD's Supper, it is again emphasized that his blood of the covenant is poured out for many (Mark 14:24). It is very clear that redemption and salvation in Christ also highlight the sealing with blood. Jesus is ultimately handed over to be crucified. At his crucifixion, even when he cries out, "My God, my God, why have you forsaken me?" (Mark 15:33), he remains bound to God. In verse 39, the officers mention clearly that this man is truly the Son of God. This is an acknowledgment of Jesus' sovereignty in Mark's Gospel.

DeSilva emphasizes that it is important to point out who Jesus Christ really was and what Jesus' service means.[9] When he refers to Mark, he first emphasizes the messianic secret that plays a very strong role in Mark, namely that there are many occasions where Jesus forbids people to talk about him because he has not yet revealed that he is the Messiah.

Luke

How must one understand Jesus Christ's sovereignty in light of the Gospel of Luke? Jesus' unique place in Luke's Gospel is strongly emphasized. When Jesus' arrival is announced, it is said that Mary was blessed. Mary then strikes up a song of praise about the promises of God who, in his

---

8. Turner, *Matthew*, 303.
9. DeSilva, *New Testament*, 201.

compassion, brings salvation and redemption to Israel. A song of praise for John the Baptist emphasizes that John the Baptist will be a prophet of the Supreme Being; that he will prepare the way for his coming, and that redemption will follow from John the Baptist's successor. Luke 2:11 emphasizes that the boy who is born will be the redeemer, Christ, the LORD. This Christ, the LORD, is the one who is glorified when the angels sing: "Glory to God in the highest heaven and on earth peace to those on whom his goodwill rests." Total salvation is already visible in Jesus Christ, but not in the way in which his death would bring salvation. Already at the temple where Simeon and Anna host Jesus, it is announced that Jesus will be a light to relieve the nations and to honor the people of Israel, and that the small child is meant to cause the fall and resurrection of many in Israel and a sign that will be denied. This strongly points out that there is already denial and that the person who comes in the sign will also be rejected. The emphasis on the separate elements is thus important.

The remarkable event of the Mount of the Transfiguration emphasizes that the Gospel of Luke also shows that the Son is the one who has an extremely unique relationship with the Father.

Acts

It is argued that Acts proffers a low Christology, and that Jesus is described as being subjected to God. There are no clear texts in which Jesus is described as eternal one with God. Acts 2:32–36, in particular, points to adoptionism. Conzelmann, however, explains that this does not mean that Luke views Jesus as subjected to God:

> This has an adoptionist ring, as if Jesus were made κύριος, "LORD," and χριστός, "Christ," only through his resurrection. For Luke Jesus was certainly Messiah during his lifetime (10:38; Luke 4:18), and he makes no essential distinction between κύριος and χριστός. Is a pre-Lukan statement of an adoptionist type reproduced here? Hardly. The formulation may come from Luke himself. Luke derives the combination of the two titles from the scriptural proof, the results of which he summarizes here; he obtains the Messiah title (vs 31) from Psalm 16 and the κύριος title from Psalm 110. Luke is not reflecting on the time of installation at all but simply sets forth God's action in opposition to the behavior of the Jews.[10]

---

10. Conzelmann, *Acts*, 21.

The witness concerning Jesus Christ in Acts does not exclude unity with God. This differs from John's Gospel. Acts 2:36 does not exclude that Jesus Christ is indeed also LORD, and that God confirms this. Bruce points to the significance of Jesus Christ as LORD and to his special relationship with YHWH (See also Acts 7:55; 9:5, 28; 10:39–43; 13:32–37; 16:31; 17:23–31; 26:15; 28:30–31; 32:8).[11] Although one must acknowledge that several of these texts point to God's confirmation of Jesus as LORD, this does not exclude the fact that he is presented as LORD who forgives sins and who is still One with God. DeSilva shows how the message about Jesus at his cross and resurrection confirms that he is the true Messiah.[12]

Bevans and Schroeder in particular point out the specific meaning of Acts.[13] The theology that comes to light is that there is a special bond with the Old Testament and the church's inclusive and universal ministry, especially in light of the prophets' behavior. The church's ministry is also based on the life and work of Jesus Christ, the LORD. The apostles' full trust that Jesus is the universal LORD and that he is also the Risen Christ is the basis of their ministry.

Summary: Synoptic Gospels and Acts

Jesus is proclaimed as the messianic King who comes into this world. He is the true Messiah, the King.[14] Jesus also reigns over all things.[15] Schreiner opines that, despite the differences, the Synoptic Gospels and Acts very clearly announce that the King has come, that Jesus of Nazareth is the Son of Man, the Son of God, the Messiah, the last Prophet, the true Israel, and LORD over everything.

The Gospel of John

John understands the way in which God acts in the world through Jesus Christ in a new manner. John assigns a totally new meaning to this. DeSilva

---

11. Bruce, *Acts*, 73–74.
12. DeSilva, *New Testament*, 361.
13. Bevans and Schroeder, *Constants in Context*, 11.
14. Schreiner, *King in His Beauty*, 474.
15. Schreiner, *King in His Beauty*, 476.

EXEGETIC AND HERMENEUTIC CONSIDERATIONS

emphasizes Jesus' death in John as the hour of his glorification.[16] According to DeSilva, the four Evangelists want to emphasize that Jesus' death is admirable. John mentions that the moment of the cross is the hour, the moment of Jesus' glorification. The cross is the beginning of his glorification. The objectionableness of the atrocious death on the cross is changed by the wonder of Jesus' salvation, which he effects at the cross and the start of his glorification. Jesus' enemies want to degrade, beat, and flagellate him. They let him carry his own wooden cross; they nail him naked to the cross. John emphasizes that Jesus meets his death willingly so that he can bring salvation and be glorified. Jesus has the authority over his own life. He hands over his own Spirit. He has a precognition of his death. He does not yield in death because his enemies are victorious. Their attempts to destroy him change as he becomes victorious. He dies in obedience to God.

This is emphasized in John's message.[17] Jesus is clearly the one who comes from above. Early Christian witness concerning Christology very distinctly emphasizes that Jesus is the one who comes from God. Several New Testament sections, such as Philippians 2:5–11; Colossians 1:15–20; 1 Timothy 3:16; and Hebrews 1:1–4, also emphasize this. Even Mark (1:1) stresses that Jesus is the Son of God. John's stronger focus and depth emphasize the relationship between Jesus and the Father.[18] The well-known *Logos* song at the beginning emphasizes this very strongly. Like the writer of Hebrews, John explored the Jewish concept of the person and work of wisdom as first evidence in terms of the truth and interpreted Jesus according to the truth. The Jewish speculation on wisdom has become a very important source for the great Christian thought about Jesus. The Fourth Evangelist wants to emphasize that Jesus is the incarnation of God, the Word, because, like wisdom, the *Logos* which John uses is the one who comes from heaven to man. There is no doubt that the Gospel of John emphasizes the fact that Jesus came to the world as the true Son of God, and that he is the LORD who comes from God.

Jesus is more than an agent. He is the sole revelation of the Father and makes the Father known in this very specific way.[19] As the only Mediator, Jesus represents God. DeSilva opines that John's presentation of Jesus relies heavily on the Jewish wisdom tradition, but that there is a very specific

16. DeSilva, *New Testament*, 427.
17. DeSilva, *New Testament*, 417.
18. DeSilva, *New Testament*, 418.
19. DeSilva, *New Testament*, 419.

emphasis of the Word of God who becomes the Mediator of God in the new creation.[20] For this reason, the Word is, according to DeSilva, the only one which the Father can reveal; the Torah or any other source can not make God known, only the Son can.

Kingship and sovereignty: Revelation

As far as Revelation is concerned, there are very clear indications of the majesty and glorification of Jesus Christ. There can be no doubt that the book of Revelation emphasizes Jesus Christ as LORD and Ruler.

The glorification of Christ is intensively emphasized in Revelation 4 and 5, where the majesty and glorification of God is very clearly stated. This must be viewed within the framework of the persecution of the believers at that time. Due to this persecution, there was the question as to whether God in his majesty indeed rules and exercises glorification.

Paul

Paul emphasizes different aspects of Jesus Christ's glorification. He determines in a very unique way the majesty and grace of Jesus Christ in what he has come to do. This is very strongly stressed in several of Paul's letters.

According to Schreiner,[21] Paul confirms that, in light of the Old Testament announcement, Jesus is the new David, and this is important for the kingship of Jesus Christ, because he is so often referred to as the Christ (375 times in Paul's writings).

Paul also confirms that Jesus' resurrection means his victory over all things. Those who belong to Jesus Christ receive the salvation which he obtained. Paul also addresses the already-and-not-yet principle very strongly. Christ has come to save his people through his cross and resurrection. This is already accomplished and will be done again at the time of salvation.[22]

Barrett opines that Paul's theology is dialectic in a paradox.[23] Paul introduces Christ in the tension of the times. Amid the various

---

20. DeSilva, *New Testament*, 419.
21. Schreiner, *King in His Beauty*, 544.
22. Schreiner, *King in His Beauty*, 579.
23. Barrett, *Paul*, 170.

announcements, crises, reformulations, and different aspects of Paul's understanding of the gospel, it is very clear that the *solus Christus* is central in his thoughts. Christ is the Crucified, with the Messiah secret as the sign of the cross. The resurrection is not a triumph, but a confirmation that the crucified Jesus is eternal and that he was crucified for those he saves.[24]

Solus Christus is the gist of Paul's theology, and justification by faith is the irrefutable truth.

Philippians

Hawthorne shows how the Christ hymn in Philippians 2:6–11 has a unique meaning in Paul's handling of Christology.[25] It has many origins, and various opinions are held as to its meaning. It is very significant that Paul emphasizes Christ's unity with God. Although it is not stated directly that Jesus Christ is God, his relationship with God is essentially expressed. The hymn means that Christ was in the form of God, "ἐν μορφῇ θεοῦ ὑπάρχων." It is difficult to explain forms, but there is a wonderful unity. Hawthorne writes:

> Thus, when this word is applied to God, his μορφή, "form," must refer to his deepest being, to what he is in himself . . . To say, therefore, that Christ existed ἐν μορφῇ θεοῦ, "in the form of God," is to say that outside his human nature Christ had no other manner of existing apart from existing "in the form of God," that is, apart from being in possession of all the characteristics and qualities belonging to God. This somewhat enigmatic expression, then, appears to be a cautious, hidden way for the author to say that Christ was God, possessed of the very nature of God.[26]

This is an exceptional expression of Christ's glorification. Hawthorne confirms this wonderful significance:

> So Phil 2:6–11 is a self-contained unit of Christian hymnody, an aretalogy in praise of the church's LORD, who becomes such as he is acknowledged by all cosmic powers as their rightful ruler. The hymn sets down the "way" he took from the Father's eternal presence, where he enjoyed the privilege of reflecting God's glory as his "image," to his ultimate glory alongside God's throne by way of his becoming human (v 7), his obedience to death (v 8), and

---

24. Barrett, *Paul*, 174.
25. Hawthorne, *Philippians*, 110–11.
26. Hawthorne, *Philippians*, 110–11.

then his being exalted to the divine throne as LORD of all creation (vv 9–11).[27]

Romans

The full significance of Paul's interpretation of Jesus Christ's unity with God has often been the subject of debates. In Paul, there are several proofs that he places Jesus Christ on the same level as YHWH: not only the word *Kurios* and the offer made in his confessions but also the whole explanation of who Jesus Christ is. It can be mentioned that some of Paul's sections could point to adoptionism, such as Romans 1:4. The question is whether Paul emphasizes that he is identified so that he can be recognized as the Son of God. This does not mean that he is not simply Son of God of eternity. The Holy Spirit simply confirms what Jesus is already, namely the Son of God in glorification. Note how this is expressed: *the Son of God who is invested with power, Jesus Christ our LORD.* This is not the language of adoptionism, but of the recognition of the glorification of Jesus.

Exoneration is achieved by *believing* in Jesus Christ (Rom 3:21). He explains that only Christ brings salvation, which is now possible because God gave Christ (Rom 3:25).

For example, in Romans 5:1, peace with God our LORD comes by believing in Jesus Christ. This again confirms the unity with God in the way in which belief in the LORD confirms this. Romans 6:4 confirms that God raised Jesus Christ, but this does not mean that unity with God is denied, because the resurrection is both the resurrection of the person Jesus and the confirmation of his divinity. Eternal life comes through Jesus (Rom 6:23). The believers are also the heirs of God in Christ (Rom 8:17). God's love is in Jesus Christ (Rom 8:39).

Romans 9:5 clearly acknowledges that Jesus is God: "Theirs are the patriarchs, and from them is traced the human ancestry of the Messiah, who is God over all, forever praised! Amen." Witherington III shows that this is a better acceptance of the Greek, that the reference refers back to Christ rather than to God.[28] Should doxology be applicable to God, this does not follow Paul's usual handling of structure. Greek grammar must emphasize that Christ's divinity is confirmed.

---

27. Hawthorne, *Philippians*, 114–15.
28. Witherington III, *Romans*, 251.

The song of praise on God's grace includes Jesus Christ (Rom 11:33–36). Romans 14:9 confirms that Jesus became alive and is the LORD of the dead and the living, to which only God has the right. Romans 15:7–13 abounds in praise to Jesus. Salvation and the grace of Christ bring salvation to the nations (Rom 15:9).

Colossians

Colossians emphasizes very strongly the glorification and majesty of Christ. The wonderful song that is viewed as an old Christian hymn (Col 1:15–20) has unique implications. First, the Son is the image of God who can not be seen, the only one that can portray God. Secondly, the Son is the origin of creation. All things originate from him. Colossians 1 conveys the message clearly. O'Brien points to the meaning of verse 15.[29] The hymn stresses that Christ must be worshipped as the loving Son who is the image of God.

Because he is the Mediator, one should not fear powers and authority. O'Brien writes:

> As the "image of the invisible God," Christ is the preexistent One who has revealed the very nature and character of God. He is both prior to and supreme over creation, for he is its LORD. All things have been created in him as the sphere and through him as the agent. Yet the passage tells us more: Christ is unique, for he is the ultimate goal of all creation (no parallel assertion was ever made of Wisdom in the OT or Jewish literature).[30]

In his summary of Paul's letters, Kim confirms that the relationship of Christ to God is portrayed in the unity with the Father, where the last Adam is the LORD who takes center stage in Paul's Christology.[31] This is closely linked with the Damascus Christophany, from which Christology developed. Paul builds his theology on what he experienced on the way to Damascus. Christ reveals himself as the image of God. Kim rejects Dunn's criticism and, for this reason, he links Christology too much with Christophany that takes place on the road to Damascus.[32]

---

29. O'Brien, *Colossians-Philemon*, 42–43.
30. O'Brien, *Colossians-Philemon*, 53.
31. Kim, *Paul*, 165.
32. Kim, *Paul*, 176.

Summary

Jesus Christ is not only acknowledged as the one with God because of the titles "Son of God," "LORD," or "Redeemer." There is abundant proof in Scripture. Nicaea is time and again confirmed.

In the New Testament, there is a strong indication of the deity of Jesus Christ. His deity must be emphasized. This means that his deity and transcendence are extremely important for any approach of mission and the way in which mission is understood.

The Three Offices of Jesus Christ

THE KINGSHIP OF JESUS CHRIST

Introduction

THIS CHAPTER DETERMINES HOW the glory of Jesus Christ has meaning in the kingdom where he rules as King. His unity with the Father means that he is the LORD. It must be determined how he rules over several domains. This is, however, a strange kingship. He is one with YHWH and therefore King who hands over power and rules differently to human kings. This chapter determines how he rules over all domains of life in a stranger way than the one who is our redemption. One must always consider Jesus Christ's unity with YHWH when determining the nature of God's rule.

The glory of Jesus Christ must, therefore, be researched thoroughly. His unity with the Father is extremely important. This also means that he is the great King. This is extremely important for mission, because the significance of his regal glory and his transcendence is very important for man to understand his specific links.

YHWH and Jesus Christ

Schreiner emphasizes that the kingship of Jesus Christ is of specific significance.[1] Although the use of the concept of "king" has been met with opposition, it is still very clear that Christ reveals himself in the world as King, as a unique person in a very unique manner. Lampe opines

---

1. Schreiner, *King in His Beauty*, 579.

that Christological titles such as "Son of God" from that time must be explained.[2] Roman emperors also bore these titles. Even as far as the Jewish approach is concerned, he opines that Moses had divine characteristics. He then wants to place the acknowledgment of the deification of Jesus in the Greco-Roman world, and not so much within the Jewish tradition of monotheism. He concludes that one must be aware of critical social and political aspects of Christology. He moves away from the acknowledgment of the substance in the unity of the relationship between Christ and God as well as from traditional titles such as "Son of God" because, according to him, this leads to misunderstanding. He opines that Jesus of Nazareth emphasized God's will and intent in order to save people. God was present in his word and deeds. For this reason, he would rather emphasize the Crucified and the poor and humble Son of God in order to talk anew about Jesus' salvation work. Although Lampe makes a significant contribution, the full relationship between Jesus and the Father can not be undervalued. Hurtado and Wright showed that Jesus Christ must be understood in light of Jewish monotheism. In light of Deuteronomy 6:4: "Hear, O Israel: The LORD our God is one LORD," he must be acknowledged; Jesus is professed as LORD, one with God. He is worshipped as LORD like the Jews worship only YHWH.[3] As the Messiah, he is the LORD who reveals YHWH fully, and he must be understood within the framework of Jewish monotheism.[4] One can not accept Lampe's proposal that the confession about Jesus must be made acceptable for modern society.

This kingship has specific missionary meaning in that it can be uniquely proclaimed in the world that Christ is King. The kingship of Christ must be proclaimed in such a way that it is never a kingship with a specific negative meaning. This kingship must always have a positive meaning. The King is the King of justice, who lets justice prevail to all, who brings salvation for all, and who, as true King, ensures redemption and salvation for all. This kingship is eternal. It ensures redemption, meaning that that there will be a new heaven and earth where the true King Christ will be. However, this King will be slaughtered as the Lamb. He condescended and brought salvation to humankind.

---

2. Lampe, "Caesar, Moses and Jesus," 9–27.
3. Hurtado, *Jesus Christ*, 30.
4. Wright, *Paul, Parts I and II*, 104.

The kingship and relationships with other religious leaders

Can Christ's glory be compared with that of Krishna of the ancestors or of Allah and Mohammed as Prophet? The question is whether one can, for instance, link Christ's life to ancestral worship. Can one talk about Christ as the Great Ancestor because he can be viewed as the living dead? A number of people emphasize this strongly, mentioning that the idea of ancestors and of Christ as the absolute ancestor does not contradict other ways in which Christ is explained and understood.[5] The concepts of *Logos*, or "Son of God," or "second Adam" can thus also point to adapting words and terms of the time when the Bible was written. This was known when the Gospels were written. It is, however, crucial that the person of Christ can be misunderstood if he is linked to the ancestors, thus totally underrating the unique work of Christ as Mediator. The way in which ancestors act as mediators must be rejected. The full implications of Christ's person, life, and work must be taken into account. Several texts in the Old Testament reject ancestral worship. One can not say that Abraham, Isaac, and Jacob are ancestors in the traditional sense of the African traditional religions, because Abraham, Isaac, and Jacob died, but live with God not as ancestors, but as people taken up by God in his glory. Jesus himself refers to this. God is not a God of the dead, but of the living. Abraham, Isaac, and Jacob live with God, not in the sense that they take over the mediator role of Christ, but that Christ remains the Mediator despite the worshipping of Abraham, Isaac, and Jacob. Ancestral worshipping leads to the acknowledgment of a mediator role among them. Christ himself is the Mediator between humans and God because, in the unity with God, he heals the broken relationship with God.

One will have to take a fresh look at the confession concerning the divinity of Christ and what this confession signifies for our understanding of the glory of God. God reveals his full glory in Christ. This is very significant for the Christian's relationship with other religions. The relationship with the African traditional religions, Islam, Hinduism, and so on, must be understood based on the confession that Christ represents the plenitude of God.

---

5. Van de Beek, *Jezus Kurios*, 197–209.

Summary

Jesus Christ is King, one with YHWH. He is, however, a totally unique king. He is the King of reconciliation and suffering. He experiences death.[6] He sacrifices himself. But he brings salvation. New things are possible through him. His kingdom is not of this world. He brings the new kingdom of God. Mission is thus always mission in humility from his reconciliation. He *is* our reconciliation, also as King. To serve such a King means that the church will be a church in humility: humble before the LORD and subservient to him but also triumphant in his glory.

JESUS CHRIST, THE TRUE PROPHET

Introduction

In respect of Christ's prophetic function, there is a special relationship between Christ as Prophet, which is linked to the Old Testament prophetic function, and the expectation that, in the new world in which we live, the church will convey a prophetic message to change people's social, economic, and political circumstances. One must establish how he as LORD acts prophetically in one's life. This section explores the significance of Jesus Christ's prophetic work in all spheres of life. From the confession that he is one with God, he claims absolute loyalty to him in all spheres of life.

Indeed, one must now explore in detail how Jesus, who is one with the Father and who must be understood in terms of his transcendence, acts in the world. He is the one who comes from God to make the world meaningful. One must consider how he does this—as the true Prophet, the persecuted Prophet and the rejected Prophet—and how he summons the world to a new relationship with him.

Old Testament perspectives

With respect to the prophetic function of Jesus Christ, one must first take note of the prophets' function in the Old Testament. These prophets received a specific calling from God. Time and again, the prophets received the word of the LORD; they were called by God himself to this function. He calls on the prophets to proclaim his word under unique circumstances.

---

6. Van de Beek, *Jezus Kurios*, 148–59.

He uses the prophets to proclaim God's radical, complete judgment and salvation. God's words call his people to radical conversion and devotion to God; a new life of devotion to God and belonging to him. They must hand themselves over to God.

Jesus Christ as true Prophet in the New Testament

Jesus is the one who is called by God to proclaim the word of God to the world. Wright points out in strong terms that Jesus must be viewed as a prophet within the framework of the second temple, namely prophets who act as prophets, so that the people to whom they bring the word can come to know that God is with them.[7] Wright covers this matter, and the specific significance of Jesus is often applied to the prophetic function. Wright does not explain the fact that salvation in Christ is more complete and wonderful than that of the prophetic function. Calvin strongly emphasized the prophetic function of Christ.[8] According to him, Christ himself is the true Prophet who proclaims the true word of God, whereby the people are called to a new relationship with God. Jesus Christ himself is thus the true Prophet who brings this redemption and salvation to the people.

A number of issues can be highlighted. First, already as a twelve-year-old, Jesus taught in the temple, thus emphasizing that he as a young child already lived in and conveyed the salvation of God, ensuring us of the fact that Jesus Christ himself would bring the prophetic word. He is the one who teaches with authority and his word comes with power.

This is further stressed in his behavior. This is emphasized more clearly when he, as second Moses, brings the new law of God in Matthew 5. Moses, the man of God, proclaimed the word of God. In Matthew 5, Jesus, as the true prophet of God, also brings God's word and message into the world. However, there is a new message. In the Sermon on the Mount, Jesus makes it very clear that he who comes from God conveys a special message to the people. In this message, Jesus clearly teaches us that true salvation lies with God himself based on our relationship with God. The glorious life depends on God and on the life in which God is the highlight and honored. This stresses that redemption and salvation lie in Christ himself and that he as Prophet, the true Prophet after Moses, can proclaim this redemption and salvation.

7. Wright, *Jesus and the Victory of God*, 147–50.
8. Calvin, *Institusie*, 11.xv.2.

Prophetic office and social relationships

Christ's prophetic function touches all aspects of life. Christ is the one who, from his prophetic words, radicalizes all social relationships to bear the relationship with Christ. From his life, one must understand how much further one needs to go. One can not understand social relationships that are not applied meaningfully based on salvation in Christ. His salvation brings new relationships that can not simply be realized on the social level. Social relationships must be renewed in Christ.

Prophetic office and politics

In line with Bloch and Marcusse,[9] some opine that Jesus Christ would create a new future and thus perpetuate revolution. Political salvation is that a perpetuating saving revolutionary state of affairs should be emphasized, and therein lies the salvation of society. One must understand that he overthrows a false order. This is viewed as the political significance of Jesus Christ, namely that he is the one who opposes their injustice and wickedness and overthrows the biased political order.

On the other hand, others state that Christ, in his redemptive grace, radicalizes this political concept of him. Christ is not a political Messiah who wants to overthrow the Romans. He would give political speeches, mentioning that Herod is a wily fox, and give his opinion about the payment of taxes, but he did not come to bring a radically new political order for the Jews by overthrowing the old political order. No. He, as suffering Servant of God, simply brings the new salvation in his name. His protest is the protest of love and is nonviolent. This may never become violent protest. Christ is the example of the nonviolent one, the one who does not act violently, but who brings salvation without violence.

The issue of total nonviolence is suddenly the order of the day. Could one then say that Christ does not approve of violence and that, from a Christian point of view, violence is thus out of the question? Should one then also say that mission always emphasizes nonviolence and that the mission and the church, in this instance, must always act nonviolently in mission? This matter must be discussed in detail. Christ's action is one of nonviolence: He does not act violently and with power; he says that those who take the sword will be destroyed; he condescends to the cross; he gives

---

9. See Verster, "Verlossingsleer," 25–29.

himself up on the cross without acting violently; he totally surrenders himself. Would this mean that believers in both mission and church should always act nonviolently? Would this then also result in a pacifist approach to all aspects of human existence in this reality? God requires justice, and the final possibility is to resist injustice with violence.

Prophetic office and science

A Christology of mission must also take serious note of the challenges that emerge in dealing with the new world in which we live. A new understanding of scientific discoveries, especially in the fields of paleontology and the origin of the universe, make strict demands of Christology. There is the issue of the origin of sin, justice, reconciliation in Christ, life and death of Christ, and the significance thereof. In terms of paleontology, a number of discoveries show that the world is considerably old, that earlier forms of existence led to later forms of existence, that there are indications of living beings who were not human beings nor apes. The way in which these issues must be interpreted is important. Many questions emerge in terms of death that formed part of reality at a very early stage of life. The interpretation of sin and its significance is also important.

Studies in paleontology strongly indicate that there was a common ancestor who produced different forms of life (ape-like or human-like). These different forms of life also have different implications for man's existence. Serious questions are raised about the existence of Adam and the way in which Adam sinned. Some query this and opine that the great story of Christianity, namely creation, the fall, and salvation, must be seriously questioned in light of modern science and that we must bid it farewell.

Dawkins attempted to show that Darwinism solved complex problems scientifically and answers the questions of the existence and origin of life and that, therefore, there is no God.[10] Science, however, has not yet solved the most essential question of life and its origin. Consequently, reality is much more complex than what Dawkins has alleged it to be.

Van de Beek makes a special distinct contribution to the debate between science and faith.[11] He shows that empirical observation can make a contribution to faith, which, in turn, can make a contribution to the empirical significance of matters. He indicates that God is not simply

10. Dawkins, *The God Delusion*, 190–200.
11. Van de Beek, *Schepping*, 46–47.

visible in the good of life as Creator but also in the brokenness of creation. God's presence in creation is simply visible in the paradox of the cross.[12] The empirical question is thus about the suffering creation. One must guard against any form of reductionism. Empirical science must also realize that science always specifically explores reality; "faith" must also realize that there is a specific way of approaching reality.[13] Reality is not straightforward; it is different and a symbolic domain of unity.[14]

One must, of course, take note of both scientific and theological discoveries that show that one must deal more cautiously with primordial creation as well as with arguments that merely proffer creationism and intelligent design such as, for example, that the earth is relatively young. On the other hand, one can not accept neo-Darwinism that neither recognizes nor accepts redemption and salvation in Christ. Redemption and salvation in Christ enable one to realize that salvation comes directly from God. These issues will have to be discussed very intensively with science. Is it possible that, in the reality where we can talk about growing development, there is a major problem, namely that the growing development often causes the most dreadful misery? What do the destructive aspects in reality reveal? Each time man attempts to bring salvation, it leads to destruction. Christology must emphasize that salvation in Christ is possible in his redeeming death. This redemption comes most intensely from his redeeming death on the cross. Christ redresses the relationship with God and makes the eschatological wonder of the new heaven and earth possible.

Prophetic office and technology

As far as mission and technology are concerned, the question is: If Christ is the LORD of all of reality, does he also control technology? The question, however, is whether we, in the modern technological society, are not surrendering to technology. Is technology taking over completely, making humans so addicted to it that they can no longer exist on their own? Humans are becoming the slave of technology that determines every aspect of life. Not only computers, tablets, and cellular phones but also the way in which technology interferes with humans and how we live accordingly cause problems. Within the technological and technocratic society, Christ

---

12. Van de Beek, *Schepping*, 47.
13. Van de Beek, *Schepping*, 55.
14. Van de Beek, *Schepping*, 81.

can liberate us so that we can apply what is available to us to the glory of his name. Christ's glory uses technology.

Prophetic office and the economy

The World Council of Churches report *Together towards Life* emphasizes the danger of worshipping mammon in the globalized world.[15] The Triune God wants to promote man's salvation in all domains, but the danger of worshipping the gods of wealth and exploitation must be pointed out. Exploitation by the great empires must be strongly rejected. Referring to *Together towards life*, Niemandt summarizes the thoughts as follows:

> The significance of "mission with creation at its heart" is that mission in God's way extends to God's creation, and that participating in life-giving mission is a crucial part of the church's mission. This entails, at the very least, missiological reflection on appropriate lifestyles and practices as part of Christian mission, and [this] means that eco-justice becomes fundamental to mission. The economic solution has moved to the centre of the stage. One of the significant effects is that poverty and affluence have diametrically grown beyond all expectations. The problem is a destructive consumerism, driving people apart. This calls for a serious reflection from the ecumenical community and creative ideas on appropriate lifestyles and practices.[16]

In conclusion, instead of the state's interference in all aspects of life in terms of greater government control and the resultant negative consequences for society, greater freedom of the market, initiative, and entrepreneurship must be promoted, so that increasingly more work opportunities can be created and totally change and renew the situation.

One must indeed guard against systems that severely affect issues such as freedom, justice, entrepreneurship, and initiative. For the Christian, these issues are most important from Christ's reconciliation. Matters such as true humaneness and true justice that one can exist as a person must be emphasized. Christ gives us the right to live, and, in our living for him, we live in all our commitments, so that we can enjoy and experience the full glory of his creation.

---

15. Keum, *Together towards Life*, 6–10.
16. Niemandt, "Towards New Life for Missiology," 95.

Prophetic office and postcolonial theology

African theologians strongly criticize the Colonial Era as well as mission as such.[17] Martey writes:

> Analysis of the African context must begin with African reality—reality which is to be located in time and space. Thus, the locus of African reality is African history. The value of history for a dispossessed people or those who have been deprived of their past can not be overemphasized. For such a people, history is an enabler that controls their lives; it prepares them to live more humanely in the present and to meet rather than to forecast the future. Rediscovery of their history deepens the sympathies, fortifies the will and liberates the mind.[18]

Others object to the way in which missionaries in Africa changed the cultural patterns of those to whom they ministered the gospel and ask serious questions about the way in which mission was practiced. It must be pointed out that many of these objections are not based on thorough recognition of the specific task and call of the gospel in the circumstances of Africa. Several aspects of the traditional uses and customs did not rhyme with the gospel of Jesus Christ. Missionaries found it impossible to bring the gospel and to merely accept the uses and customs such as, for example, the killing of twins or specific marriage customs that degrade women, which are in conflict with the gospel.

It must also be pointed out that the concept of "gospel" is often modelled on a Western approach, and that specific uses and customs of the indigenous people of Africa are not always acknowledged and developed in a way that could be supported by the gospel. This approach often led to disregarding the specific development of a community in that way. The atrocities of colonialism and the misdeeds of apartheid must be acknowledged at all costs. A South American perspective points out several aspects of colonialism and its destructive effects. Post-colonialism wants to react to this.[19] Pears points to the fact that, since the 1980s, postcolonialism has been regarded as a series of theories, approaches, and literary techniques

---

17. See Mugambi, *African Christian Theology*, 1–152; Setiloane, *African Theology*, 1–35; Oduyoye, *Christianity in Africa*, 1–147; Martey, *African Theology*, 1–190.

18. Martey, *African Theology*, 36.

19. Quijano, "Coloniality and Modernity/Rationality." 168–78; Quijano and Ennis, "Coloniality of Power, Eurocentrism, and Latin America," 533–80.

in order to question power structures and address inequalities.[20] She also points out that postcolonial theology reacts to the offences of colonialism. Pears writes:

> Whilst keeping a sense of the diversity that are postcolonial theologies, postcolonial theology can nevertheless be characterized as incorporating a strong sense of multiple Christian identities and of human subjectivity, as rejecting a homogenous Christian voice as representative of global Christianity and as challenging, universalizing tendencies in Christian scholarship. Postcolonial theologies are subversive of even their own positions and approaches and are concerned to continually question and critically interrogate.[21]

Postcolonial theology very strongly opposes colonialism. Postcolonial theology wants to be a theology for Africa, for the people of Africa, and a theology from Africa itself, to provide meaningful answers for the people of Africa.

There are various reasons for the development of postcolonial theology. First, one must acknowledge that the Colonial Era was not always in the best interests of Africa. Although colonial development influenced the development of infrastructure, medical care, hospitals, schools, and churches considerably, it often also meant that raw materials in the communities, where the colonial areas settled, were taken away from the people and not used for their own benefit. Such exploitation can not be accepted under any circumstances.

Secondly, people's own circumstances must have an answer to theology. Oduyoye explains this as follows:

> African theologians have moved from debates about what African theology is, or is not, and from discussions of what it might become. The period of advising others on what to do in order to give birth to an authentic and relevant African theology is moving to one of expression of faith by Africans who have had formal theological education with all the scientific disciplines that it involves.[22]

Bosch strongly states that this emphasizes the idea of inculturation and contextualization.[23] It must be understood that, under specific circum-

---

20. Pears, *Contextual Theology*, 133.
21. Pears, *Contextual Theology*, 164.
22. Oduyoye, *Christianity in Africa*, 147.
23. Bosch, *Transforming Mission*, 420–32, 447–57.

stances, it is very important to bring the gospel to the people to enable them to answer to it from their own situation and that this answer can be significantly understood. Such answers have intensive meaning for how people can understand the gospel. The agents differ. In the Colonial Era, it was thought that the missionary must use the Western approach to mission. Instead, a new approach must be followed where the receivers of the message provide the answers. Answers must be formulated for themselves. Setiloane explains that a unique African theology from their own understanding of God is essential: "But it [African theology] calls for more. It denounces and frees itself from the very foundations of Western Theology. The battle is not against the Faith or Kerygma, rather it is against Western accretions which are now turned into Dogma."[24]

The gospel must be in the community and provide an answer for those within that specific community. Mugambi writes:

> This challenge clearly points to a new change of relationships, the exaltation of the powerless, and the wilful abandoning of power by the powerful in humility so that humanity may achieve dignity. If the powerful will not wilfully acknowledge the desire of the powerless to share political power and the power of the cross, then God will empower the powerless, and the first may become last while the last may become first. But the reversal of roles and status is not ideal. The ideal is a renewal of society so that a new creation comes into being, a new creation in which political power and the power of the cross are at equilibrium.[25]

Postcolonial theology became significant because it developed theology in communities where there was hardly any talk of theologizing in answer to what Scripture says.

Postcolonial theology is also significant for the Western world that must understand that the theologizing of the West is not the only way. People practice theology within their specific circumstances. The Western approach must thus be adapted to meet the circumstances of other nations. Lastly, the West must also realize that many mistakes have been made and that, in many respects, sin was also committed in the way in which the church existed in Africa.

It is important to develop a reformatory approach. Postcolonial theology expressed animosity against and rejection of Western influence. This

---

24. Setiloane, *African Theology*, 35.
25. Mugambi, *African Christian Theology*, 120.

often also meant that the gospel was rejected and that they did not listen to the significance of Jesus Christ's sovereignty. Despite great progress and democratization, postcolonial Africa is still, in many respects, in the deepest misery. A civil war is still waging in South Sudan. Zimbabwe's dictatorial government suppresses its people. There is severe misery in Congo and other areas. The signs of new hope in countries such as Namibia, Botswana, and Ghana must be cherished, but there are still numerous challenges.

Reformatory theology would also point out the misuses of the colonial times and apartheid while taking seriously the misery and enormous need of people in Africa. This needs solutions against dictatorships, corruption, and exploitation of people. In theologizing about Jesus Christ, one will have to emphasize that he is the one from whom, through whom, and to whom all things are. His glory, his sovereignty, his unity in the Triune God must be emphasized. Christ will be acknowledged for who he really is, and one will have to ignore the concept that Christ is simply a potential prophet. He who has come to bring us his glory must in all respects be glorified.

The church in Africa will have to turn afresh to Jesus Christ as LORD. Jesus Christ's sovereignty over every aspect of life is essential. His sovereignty from the church over all aspects of life must be emphasized. What is the meaning of Jesus Christ in this respect for all?

Christ's prophetic function will have to be highlighted in a reformatory theology. People will not be able to shift their responsibility onto others and thus not take the responsibility for their own deeds. Dictatorial rulers will have to be called to account. The church as suffering church in Africa under the cross must stand up and say that we can not at all accept this rejection of Jesus Christ and his sovereignty, and the corruption. In Africa, there will have to be signs of the salvation of Christ that asks responsibility of all people. This can only happen if responsibility is taken in terms of the economy.

Prophetic office and mission

This prophetic function is of particular significance for mission. On the missionary level, it affects all forms of man's existence, but because of this, it must always be viewed with reference to Jesus Christ. The prophetic function must remain linked to Jesus Christ, and the salvation he brings must be viewed radically in the relationship with him and his significance for people. The salvation he brings creates new possibilities of redemption, blessing, and a new future. The prophet also proclaims the new time again and again. When the prophet announces the new time, salvation will emerge. When this happens, the wonder of the new time will also be experienced meaningfully. The prophet announces that there will be judgment and punishment and that salvation will be visible in a new world. This salvation will then have to be significantly conveyed in society. In his life, death, and resurrection, Christ as Prophet announces the new salvation. From a prophetic point of view, the church is called upon to share in Christ's prophetic function and thus convey the salvation which he proclaims to people.

It is significant for mission that it must be approached from the prophetic function of Jesus Christ. This means that he as Prophet, as the transcendent Prophet, must be viewed not only as a prophet of this world, but also as the one who brings new salvation and establishes a new kingdom. This salvation and kingdom come from above. This wonder can only be recognized in light of what Jesus Christ experienced. His wonder and glory will then ultimately be significant. Thus, salvation comes to the world. This Prophet, Jesus Christ, who as Broken and Crucified Man brings us salvation through death, has meaning for mission in all these different aspects. Mission thus becomes a new witness concerning him who renews all aspects of life. This always happens in brokenness and in service of the LORD.

JESUS, THE GREAT HIGH PRIEST

Introduction

As Priest, Jesus Christ is the one who reaches out to humans. It must, therefore, be established how he as Son of God and as human being accomplishes the priestly task. He hands himself over. The significance of reconciliation is thus very important. The events of salvation in his life must also be considered. As one with God, he is the one who fulfils the priestly role. More than ever, it must now also be acknowledged that he as Priest is humans' reconciliation. This section explores this matter in detail. His life is proof of salvation. The different aspects of his life indicate why he is our reconciliation. Of great importance in the approach to the priestly role of Jesus Christ is that one must explore how Christ, as the great High Priest, hands himself over. In this instance, one must inquire as to the significance of the wonderful word that Jesus Christ is our redemption.

This reconciliation is significant for humans in all the different aspects of their lives. Jesus is the great High Priest, the one who, in many spheres and through his incarnation, brings salvation in this world. One must, therefore, inquire as to the significance of the broken High Priest who gives himself over for total redemption. This occurs in all the different aspects of salvation which he brings, so that it can be acknowledged as the way in which he brings redemption to man.

One for others

Christ is the Priest *par excellence*, the one who intervenes for the sake of others. As the great High Priest, he is the one who obtains salvation and redemption for others. This is more clearly emphasized in Hebrews, which unequivocally states that the priest order of Melchizedek is above that of Aaron. This priest order is from the beginning of time, and Melchizedek is described as a man greater than the ancestor Abraham because offerings were made to him.

The relationship between Christ and the Levitical priesthood is further discussed in the Hebrew letter. Christ is described as the one, according to the order of Melchizedek, who is from a higher order of priesthood and that he as priest brings the final offer, once and for all. He has become the offer of the greater salvation.

Christ's high priesthood highlights the specific ministry of prayer. Not only did he often isolate himself to pray, but his prayers bear profound messages. His prayers reveal salvation for the community and for the people of God. Christ's prayer in Gethsemane is the climax of his priesthood, where he calls to God to let the cup pass from him. He accepts God's will, because, as Priest, he acts in and confirms the new covenant. He hands himself over in order to establish the new covenant. In Gethsemane, he hands himself over obediently. He is prepared to be offered for the sake of others. This aspect of the priestly behavior of Jesus has specific significance for missionary Christology: Christ as the one for the sake of others who offers himself for the sake of others. He devotes himself, and he is the one who hands himself over, but he also acts for others and, by doing so, he makes it possible in mission to make God's salvation visible.

The witness in Deuteronomy 18:5 is fulfilled in Jesus, as the Priest in the line of the Levites.

Only Jesus Christ is our full redemption

The significance of missionary Christology is important in terms of the various actions of Christ and the events of salvation in Christ's life.

In *Transforming Mission*, Bosch explains that salvation is significant for man's redemption in Christ's various actions.[26] The missionary significance of incarnation, the life of Christ, his death on the cross, his resurrection, his ascension and return, and the glorification by the Holy Spirit are important. It is thus important to explore in more detail each one of these different aspects of Christ's salvation activities.

The birth of Christ

The birth of Jesus Christ is associated with the word "Immanuel," God with us. His birth is especially significant, as confirmed in Matthew 1:22: the one who is to be born will be named Jesus, so that the Word which the LORD said via the prophet will be accomplished.

The virginal conception emphasizes the absolute uniqueness of Jesus in that he is God near or with us. At the birth, other aspects emerge in the Christology of mission, as in the Gospel of Luke. Brown emphasizes the scriptural proof that confirms the virginal conception.[27] This confirms both Jesus' unique humanness and his uniqueness as Son of God. Brown writes that Mary's virginity must continuously be discussed, but that the wonder should not be undervalued:

> Moreover, there is the danger that the discussion might imperil a traditional formulation of faith that has served Christianity well, and those who discuss the matter must show a sensitivity for the underlying beliefs that have been formulated in terms of virginal conception.[28]

The concept of "deep incarnation" means that Jesus Christ's incarnation includes the entire creation and not only humanity. Gregersen also emphasizes that Christ's incarnation must be totally confirmed in discussions in religious studies.[29] According to him, the *Logos* not only accepted

---

26. Bosch, *Transforming Mission*, 393–400.
27. Brown, *Virginal Conception and Bodily Resurrection of Jesus*, 61–65.
28. Brown, *Virginal Conception and Bodily Resurrection of Jesus*, 67.
29. Gregersen, "Deep Incarnation and Kenosis," 251–52.

humanity but also the total matrix of materiality. According to this view, there must be continuity of humaneness with animals and the material world in its "growth, vulnerability, and decay." The fleshliness of Jesus Christ thus includes the whole dimension of materiality. Gregersen writes:

> What deep incarnation adds to these many prepositions is the little "as." God appears as a human person in Jesus Christ (so also Luther), but in such depth, I would add, that in Jesus Christ the entire matrix of materiality is assumed in his blood and body. Incarnation does not only refer to a general presence of God in the midst of the world (there are many other temporary divine embodiments such as burning bushes, temples, or prophets). The point is that the Eternal Son is appearing as flesh in the life story of Jesus from cave to cross. With the resurrection of Jesus through the life-giving power of the divine Spirit also the humanity of Jesus (and in him the whole assumed cosmos) gains a permanent place in the eternal divine life.[30]

Jesus is thus also bound to ecology. Niemandt emphasizes the significance of deep incarnation for mission.[31] Just as God's eternal *Logos* becomes man and shares in human life, Christ is further incarnated in creation itself. God even shares the lowest forms of life by sharing in the biological life. God not only became human in Jesus Christ, but he also became part of the natural world by his incarnation in all evolutionary processes and developments.[32] Although it must be emphasized that Jesus became fully human in real life, the proponents of deep incarnation totally overestimate materiality. The question is whether this misjudges the unique place of Jesus in the incarnation.

Jesus Christ's earthly life

Christ's life is the second aspect to be strongly emphasized. His behavior from birth to death has significance for the whole of human existence, as emphasized in Matthew 4:23.

Jesus' significance as the healing wonderful LORD was emphasized earlier. In his acts as person on earth, he is the one who heals, who brings salvation, and who guarantees wonderful things for humans. He is the one

---

30. Gregersen, "Deep Incarnation and Kenosis," 252.
31. Niemandt, "Missiology and Deep Incarnation," 249–50.
32. Niemandt, "Missiology and Deep Incarnation," 250.

who makes this possible, because he came from God as Son of God. He performs miracles, he heals the paralyzed, the blind, those who are ill. He performs miracles such as multiplying the bread; he walks on the sea so that his glory can be confirmed over the whole world and so that people can see what special significance must be given to him.

Christ's life in the missionary acts of the church thus has unique significance for each one who would come to him.

Berkhof strongly emphasized Jesus, in historical life, as human being among other human beings.[33] Jesus' words and deeds concretize his Sonship. Berkhof uses various terms to explain the humanness of Jesus: love for the Father, obedience to the Father, and that Jesus represents God to people in establishing the covenant.[34] Jesus himself is the embodiment of the covenant, with his radical forgiveness and mercy. This is associated with the freedom to which he calls people. He emphasizes the cheerfulness of life before God, where the kingdom must be sought. The freedom that Jesus brings also includes nature. Berkhof chooses the term "humanity" rather than "sinlessness" to emphasize God's intention with man.[35] The sinlessness of Jesus must, however, still be emphasized.

The crucifixion

Berkhof opines that the earthly life of Jesus, which ends in his death, brings the kingdom of God close to people and that, in this offer, he completes and fully reveals new humanness.[36] His suffering and death mean his continuous and complete being together with people for the sake of God and with God for the sake of man. Berkhof uses the words "representant" and "representative," because Jesus as Mediator brings humans reconciliation with God.[37]

Welker explains that the cross proclaims not only the suffering Christ, not even the suffering God but also the God of justice and the God who saves.[38] The cross reveals the terrible Godforsaken situation of humanity, in which people act for fear, anxiety, and aggression towards God's presence in

33. Berkhof, *Christelijk Geloof*, 309.
34. Berkhof, *Christelijk Geloof*, 311–13.
35. Berkhof, *Christelijk Geloof*, 313.
36. Berkhof, *Christelijk Geloof*, 315.
37. Berkhof, *Christelijk Geloof*, 319.
38. Welker, *God the Revealed: Christology*, 185–90.

life. It also reveals the depth of sin and God's suffering in which he reveals his nearness to humans. Even God's godliness is questioned in the cross, but the relationship between Creator, Spirit, and Jesus Christ is revealed. In the power of the Spirit, the hopeless situation changes into one of hope. One can not misjudge Jesus Christ's death of atonement.

As far as the priestly function in terms of the crucifixion is concerned, various aspects are strongly emphasized. As Priest and LORD, he has given his life. Many questions are raised concerning the issue of the offer of Christ. Did he suffer as a substitute and thus offer his life so that we can be saved by his offer of death on the cross? He hands himself over so that he can bring our salvation and redemption. He does so by offering himself on the cross. Paul points out that Jesus was given as an offer in order to effect redemption. Second Corinthians 5:11–21 discusses the question of whether Jesus' death on the cross was a sacrifice and whether he proclaimed himself ambassador.

This world and the present do not have the final answer. One can indeed ask, "What about the thousands of Christians throughout the ages who were persecuted and killed, who did not experience salvation on earth, but who expected salvation in the redemption that he would effect?" One must emphasize the redemption work of Jesus Christ. The church as missional church must thus convey to people a total spectrum of the salvation in Jesus Christ. He brings complete salvation not only for this world but also for the world hereafter; not only now but also in the future. The world is not our home, because this world passes by. Our home is in Christ, and our salvation is to be found in him.

In his book *The Non-Violent Atonement*, Weaver challenges Anselm's theology of substitution.[39] He opines that violence is the underlying theological framework of the theology of substitution and that it can no longer be maintained. He wants to further develop the idea of Christ Victor. The classic Christ Victor model determines that the ransom be paid to the devil and not to God. He joined various theologians who want to avert the violent element from substitution.

> Narrative Christ Victor is indeed atonement if one means a story in which the death and resurrection of Jesus definitively reveal the basis of power in the universe, so that the invitation from God to participate in God's rule—to accept Jesus as God's anointed one—overcomes the forces of sin and reconciles sinners to God.

---

39. Weaver, *Non-Violent Atonement*, 197.

Through identification with Jesus, sinful humankind shares in Jesus' death and his resurrection. To identify with Jesus is to have life in the reign of God.[40]

The classic substitution text is 2 Corinthians 5:11–21. Substitution and participation imply God's love.[41] The God of love acts according to his principles and can thus not be accused of violence on the human level. Harris describes reconciliation as follows:

> As a Pauline theological term depicting the relationship of God with humans, "reconciliation" denotes a transformation of relations, not in the sense that the original friendly relations are restored (humans are by nature in enmity with God, Rom 5:10; Eph 2:1–3) but in the sense that friendly relations now replace former hostility. Reconciliation restores humans to a proper relationship with God (the vertical aspect) and with fellow human beings (the horizontal aspect), just as sin produces in humans a twofold alienation, from God and from other human beings.[42]

Matthias points out that, for Luther's classic understanding of Christology, the relationship between the person and the work of Jesus Christ is the presence of the person of Jesus Christ, of redemption, whereas, for the Reformers in the classic Reformed understanding of Christology, Jesus is the Mediator of redemption.[43] Matthias also wants to emphasize that there is a difference in the relationship between the divine and the human nature of Christ. The concept of Christ's deity is important for the relationship between his divine and human nature.

Salvation in Christ is so wonderful that it can not be placed under one denominator. Paul's mission was to confirm the significance of substitution and participation. He did so throughout his life. He did not imply what he understood by this, namely that God acts violently towards his own son. He wanted to establish the transition to new life and new time in Christ.

Proceeding from this is the idea that Christ's salvation and reconciliation is, in fact, associated with the salvation of human beings who participate in his suffering. This is the model of participation; Christ dies on the cross, but people participate in this suffering and this form of redemption. This is in line with Romans 6. Paul mentions that people are interred with

---

40. Hahn, *Theologiegeschichte des Urchristentums*, 220.
41. Weaver, *Non-Violent Atonement*, 45.
42. Harris, *Second Epistle to the Corinthians*, 436.
43. Matthias, "'Lutheran' Christology in Barth's Doctrine of Justification," 20.

him through baptism. In Romans 6:5–8, he states that he/she will also be restored to life with Christ.

The resurrection

Welker discusses whether Jesus' resurrection was simply a vision or a myth.[44] Should one ascribe a specific historicity to this? Welker points out that the New Testament witness about the empty grave and the apparition is not unambiguous.[45] This conveys a complex historical reality. But it is very clear that there was the conviction that he truly died and was raised from the dead so that his living presence is a reality. Through the power of the Spirit, the post-Easter Jesus makes himself known gradually in greater glory. Welker confirms the reality of the resurrection as follows:

> This event is as little an "illusion" as was the discovery of mathematics, music, or justice. It is not merely that a new order of things, a new sphere of knowledge or experience, has been disclosed; it is the person and life of Jesus that comes to bear in a new and different fashion, so much so that Paul can now speak of a "spiritual body" (1 Cor. 15:44).[46]

His reference to N. T. Wright's point of view is also very important. This view emphasizes that Jesus was not only alive again, but that he historically became physically alive. Although Welker acknowledges that it is important to show that the reality of the resurrection may not be misjudged,[47] he still wants to consider the full implication of all the versions and of Paul, in particular, and he wants to consider the resurrection in light of the Spirit's presence in Jesus.[48]

Christ's resurrection is a climax of the salvation events. Berkhof describes this as the definitive salvation event.[49] The resurrection guarantees life after death, and therefore it is so meaningful in 1 Corinthians 15. Paul writes that, according to the gospel, Christ was raised from the dead, and that Christ died for our sins, according to the Scriptures. He was

---

44. Welker, *God the Revealed: Christology*, 104.
45. Welker, *God the Revealed: Christology*, 119.
46. Welker, *God the Revealed: Christology*, 126.
47. Welker, *God the Revealed: Christology*, 128.
48. Welker, *God the Revealed: Christology*, 142.
49. Berkhof, *Christelijk Geloof*, 324.

buried, and on the third day he was raised from the dead, according to the Scriptures. He did appear, but then he uttered the important statement in 1 Corinthians 15:12.

Crossan follows an interesting approach.[50] He opines that, in light of the expectation of the martyrs' resurrection in the time between the Testaments (Maccabean), the expectation and conviction in the New Testament is that Jesus will "physically" resurrect. This is what the Jews were expecting at that time. Crossan believes that the early Christians simply applied this to Jesus. According to Crossan, this can not happen, and it is not true, but Jesus' followers used it. One must agree with Crossan that the resurrection is understood as physical. By contrast, one must confess with Paul that, if Christ is not resurrected, our faith is worthless (1 Cor 15:12–19).

From a missional point of view, this means that the redemption in Christ has specific significance for all aspects of life. It fills life from all aspects. It means the sense of life. Christ's resurrection is significant in the most critical circumstances. This creates hope, which is the full salvation obtained in Christ. This salvation is significant for eternity and for humans' existence. This ensures that God's salvation will become a reality and will be completely fulfilled. This fulfilment, this salvation, is significant for every person who is in Christ. The resurrection assures the expectation of the new heaven and the new earth, where the risen man will serve God in glory and live to eternity. The resurrection is the assurance that Christ's salvation events are not in vain. From a missional point of view, this means that the church can also proceed to proclaim the incredible message of redemption in this world.

Life after death

Currently, there is much doubt about the existence of heaven and hell. Numerous sectors raise the question as to whether one can at all believe in a superreality such as heaven, where people will live in bliss and experience the joy of this bliss with God. On the other hand, the concept of "hell" is associated with premodern primitive thought, as if there is a place where people are martyred forever because they have committed one or other sin. Heaven and hell are approached radically differently from various angles. The question increasingly arises as to whether it is still really meaningful to address this in a missional approach. Can one still talk about heaven

---

50. Crossan, "Resurrection of Jesus," 29–57; Crossan, *Historical Jesus*, 395–423.

and hell in modern times? What is the answer to this from a missional perspective?

In considering heaven and hell, it is essential to refer to sources. To evaluate these perspectives, one must scrutinize exegetic, hermeneutic, dogmatic, and ethical approaches from Scripture. Lebhar opines that the unique image of heaven and the promise of life after death are fundamental to Christian faith.[51] Moore points out that there are different opinions on the concept of hell.[52] In particular, the idea that God will judge and punish people is viewed as an unacceptable human action. God could prevent injustice and does not need to punish.

As far as the views on hell are concerned, Moore shows that there are a number of different views thereof in the Christian world.[53] One view understands hell literally as the punishment of God's fair eternal judgment (See Tertullian, Augustine, and Jonathan Edwards). Another view is that the punishment and suffering in hell is unknown.[54] Calvin, F. F. Bruce, and Billy Graham opine that the images in the Bible emphasize the serious nature of the matter without literally describing the judgment. The nihilists opine that the second death points to those who will not survive, but rather be eradicated. Eternal life is for the faithful. The concept of "immortal soul" is accordingly Hellenistic (Clemens Origines, C. S. Lewis, and John Stott advocate this idea).[55]

Van de Beek points out that the Bible mentions definite rejection in various ways.[56] Hell is a place of crying and grinding of teeth, of inextinguishable fire, where worms never die, and there is a pool of fire and sulphur, the place of torment (See Matt 8:12; 13:42; 13:24, 51; 25:30; 26:45; Luke 13:28; 16:23; Mark 9:43, 48; Rev 19:20; 20:14; 21:8; Jude 13).

Although the New Testament points to judgment comprehensively and to grace profusely, salvation is never universal. Those who are lost are always called to life in terms of God's appeal for love and redemption. According to Exalto, Paul points out that he is yearning to be with Christ.[57] This includes an immediate conscious uniting with Christ after death.

---

51. Lebhar, "Heaven," 259.
52. Moore, "Hell," 301.
53. Moore, "Hell," 302.
54. Moore, "Hell," 302.
55. Moore, "Hell," 303–04.
56. Van de Beek, *Eschatologie als Christologie*, 104.
57. Exalto, "Sterven en dan . . ." 565.

Earthly relationship with Christ is incomplete; after death, he will obtain complete relationship with him. There is thus a yearning for heavenly bliss after death.

Dogmatically, the key question is the issue of theodicy. Who is God? What must one say of God in this respect? It must be emphasized that God is holy. In his self-revelation in both the Old and the New Testaments, God makes himself known as the Holy One who does not tolerate sin. In addition, humans are totally guilty before God. As clearly indicated, God is the God of Love. Justice and love must thus be acknowledged in all respects. God's judgment is inevitable, but it is dealt with anew in his love. Romans 5 teaches that grace is more profuse than sin. The impossible has occurred in that God saves through himself. From his very nature, God is known as love. The wonder of God's love must be profusely proclaimed. Salvation and redemption are always associated with new birth and faith. God's love is his love in justice that is provided by faith in Jesus Christ.

Ascension

Ascension assures accession to the throne of the LORD who hands himself over, of the Lamb that is slaughtered, not the one who wants to rule with sovereignty and self-righteousness.[58] It is the accession to the throne of the Broken one, of the one who offers us glory in brokenness. Ascension is the assurance that the resurrection is complete. In the full sense of the word, resurrection is finalized, and ascension assures us of the fact that it did occur.

The return

The salvation that ultimately breaks through is the salvation that comes from God. The eschatological Christ is the one who was raised from the dead and who ensures our resurrection. This reconciliation and redemption will also mean reconciliation and redemption for us. This reconciliation is significant for those who believe in him because he will return. In terms of the eschatological expectation of Christ's return, Wright writes that salvation in Christ will occur at the time of resurrection and that resurrection will be complete for those who find salvation in him.

---

58. Van de Beek, *Jezus Kurios*, 172–73.

The expectation that the LORD will come and that he will fulfil his salvation and that redemption will be finalized creates new hope. From a missional perspective, this means that Christ, who was crucified, who was raised from the dead, and who ascended to heaven will finalize total salvation—the eschatological salvation—and ultimately unite all aspects of salvation. The wonder of salvation will be visible in Christ. When he returns, those who expect him in his glory will experience its wonder.

SUMMARY

The Great High Priest humbled himself. He comes into the world as the Broken One due to the fact that he bears the sin of man. He brings God's salvation transcendently because he is the wonderful Son of God. As eternal Son of God, he facilitates salvation in handing himself over. Mission must proclaim this. Mission must emphasize that Jesus Christ as Great High Priest is the one of our reconciliation. He brings salvation as he hands himself over. He brings redemption because he is the one for the other. Mission must always emphasize this. Jesus Christ must always be acknowledged as the LORD of church and society.

The Holy Spirit

THE PERSON AND WORK OF THE HOLY SPIRIT

THE PERSON AND WORK of the Holy Spirit is definitively of interest to mission. Not only the confession that the Holy Spirit is truly God and one of the persons of the Trinity but also the acknowledgment of his work in the church for the salvation of many, are undeniably wonderful. Indeed, the Holy Spirit effects rebirth and conversion in people. The soteriological work of the Holy Spirit is of great importance for mission. The Holy Spirit as the Spirit of Christ facilitates mission, builds the church, glorifies Christ, emphasizes and bears the unity of the church, as well as guides the church in being involved in the world. This work of the Spirit also gives new significance to mission. The Holy Spirit sends out the church to proclaim, confess, and propagate the full confession that Jesus is truly the Savior of the world.

After the section on Christology, this section is about the Holy Spirit. This is followed by referring to the wonder of the love of the Father. The Father's love is visible through the work of the Holy Spirit in Jesus Christ. Through his love, the Father determines the work of the church. The missional work of the church is in service to God the Father through the Holy Spirit in Jesus Christ. The love of the Father for those who sin is thus central in the theology of mission. The sections on Christ, on the wonderful Holy Spirit, and on the Father of love complement each other. This presents a Trinitarian theology of mission.

Who is the Holy Spirit, and how should one understand his work? Should one emphasize the cosmological work of the Holy Spirit? Does it occur as such in the Bible? What is the relationship between the Spirit and Christ, and how should one understand this relationship? Does the Spirit reveal sin, and how should one react to this? What is the specific significance of confession, in terms of the Holy Spirit, for mission? How does the work of the Spirit manifest in the church? Reconciliation with God is essential. How does the Spirit effect this reconciliation? Do both the Old and the New Testaments attest to the person and work of the Holy Spirit? How does the Old Testament attest to the work of the Holy Spirit?

The aim of this part is to explore what is understood by the person and the unique work of the Holy Spirit and its significance for mission and the wonder of God's love. The Holy Spirit as Spirit of Christ and as person in the Trinity is essentially important when considering mission. The work of the Holy Spirit is often understood superficially when it is associated with mission. Emotional outbursts are not the way in which the Spirit works. It is necessary to point out why it is not understood as such. The role of the Holy Spirit in the church and how the Spirit empowers the church to be involved in mission is also important when considering the Spirit and mission. The question as to the work of the Holy Spirit beyond the church is also important for mission and must be taken into account. Is there also mention of the cosmological work of the Holy Spirit?

In the New Testament, the Spirit's profound relationship with Christ is obvious. It is thus essential to consider how the Holy Spirit glorifies Christ. One must investigate that close link in order to determine whether the Spirit also works beyond the church. Is there talk of the Spirit's work in other religions, and what is the nature of that work? Does the Spirit also bring salvation in other religions? The unity of the Holy Spirit and Christ is, in this instance, of great importance. The question is whether it includes or excludes. These questions are of great importance to mission.

What is the role of the Holy Spirit in eschatology? This matter also deserves specific attention. Does the Spirit prepare only for eternity, or is the Spirit also working for the coming of Christ? In this instance, one will have to understand that the concept of "eternity" is understood differently. Realized eschatology already includes aspects of salvation, but a future aspect must also be emphasized. The here-and-now is now the final answer.

One must guard against a straightforward link between *ruach* in the Old Testament and the Holy Spirit. Although theologians such as Jonker[1] and Heyns[2] opine that there are clear mentions of the presence of the Holy Spirit in the Old Testament, Vos indicates that various Old Testament experts point out that there is no such concept of the Holy Spirit in the Old

---

1. Jonker, *Die Gees van Christus*, 121–22.
2. Heyns, *Dogmatiek*, 294.

Testament, where the Only God is set against idols.³ This does not mean that the Trinity does not appear in the Old Testament, but that only God is revealed as God in the New Testament. Vos shows that *ruach* is the work of God. It is thus important not to link *ruach* in Genesis 1:2 directly with the Holy Spirit.

Vos describes the significance of the Spirit (*ruach*) in the Old Testament. First, the monotheistic approach of the Old Testament makes it impossible to consider the Spirit as dependent on or separate from God. Secondly, we must confirm the relationship between the Spirit (*ruach*) and the Messiah. YHWH sends the Messiah to fulfil his task. The Messiah must realize God's rule of law. The Messiah confirms that God is God (the only proof of God), and YHWH's sovereignty as King is directed at Israel and the people. God equips the Messiah with his Spirit in order to fulfil this task. The full sovereignty of the Messiah is kept under cover in the Old Testament, but it is revealed in Christ in the New Testament.⁴ Thirdly, the Spirit's wholehearted re-creation of life facilitates the re-creation of God's people. The Spirit also gives hope for the people in this life. This is also understood in a cosmic way. Fourthly, God's work of re-creation also has a cosmic aspect.⁵

Vos mentions that the Spirit in the Old Testament is not the hypostasis of God, but that the *ruach* indicates God-in-action or God himself. This does not mean that, if the Old Testament does not mention the Spirit as a person, then there is also no link with the Holy Spirit in the New Testament, and that the background of the Old Testament is not significantly taken into account in the New Testament.⁶

A number of theologians agree with Vos, indicating that the Spirit in the Old Testament is not mentioned as the Third Person of the Trinity. Tribe writes:

> The spirit, then, has no personality of its own, but is a power emanating from God and operated by Him, whether in the sphere of nature or of supernature. There is thus no hint or foreshadowing of the doctrine of the third person of the Trinity. We have seen that there is in the Old Testament both a continuous regular

---

3. Vos, "Heilige Gees," 83.
4. Vos, "Heilige Gees," 94.
5. Vos, "Heilige Gees," 103.
6. Vos, "Heilige Gees," 107.

development of the doctrine of the spirit and separate unconnected beliefs as to its power and working.[7]

He does indicate that Paul records specific developments. According to Burton,

> Beginning undoubtedly as a term of physical or dynamic meaning, denoting wind, was already early in the literary period a religious term in the sense that it was used in connection with the idea of God to denote the invisible power by which he operated in the world, or for God himself as operative, but not for a hypostasis distinct from God.[8]

Davies confirms this:

> The dominant description of the Spirit in the Old Testament is essentially a power as distinct from the ever-increasing sense of the personality and person of the Spirit in the New Testament. Of course, in the Old Testament there is an approach to the personification of the Spirit as in Isaiah 63:10.[9]

Kaiser explains his point of view as follows:

> The indwelling presence of the Holy Spirit is defined as the abiding and ongoing work of the Holy Spirit of God, in which he resides within the believer to bless or to judge each, as determined by the standard of God's covenant and will. This is to be distinguished from God's omnipresence and his work in the physical realms, or even in his occasional presence when he was "with" one such as Ishmael (Gen 21:20), which does not carry the full benefits of his presence as it did, for example, with Isaac (Gen 26:3), the person of promise. Once again, we must ask: If the regenerating work of the Holy Spirit enabled Old Testament persons to believe, as most appear to readily agree, how were these old covenant saints maintained and established in their faith if they were not indwelt by God's Spirit?[10]

---

7. Tribe, "The Spirit in the Old Testament Writings," 268–69.
8. Burton, "Spirit, Soul, and Flesh," 77.
9. Davies, "The Holy Spirit in the Old Testament," 134.
10. Kaiser, "Holy Spirit in the Old Testament," 309.

Further,

> We conclude, then, that the Holy Spirit did indwell Old Testament believers. The promise of the Spirit that was new was their incorporation into the universal Church, the Body of Christ.[11]

The Spirit is associated with God's powerful work and does not have his own personality alongside God.

Dumbrell refers to the fact that the Spirit works in humans and that the Old Testament confirms the Spirit's work.[12] The Spirit, however, works in humans' heart to place the law of God. This occurs only in the New Testament, but God already works in the heart of people in the Old Testament.

It is obvious that the Spirit (*ruach*) in the Old Testament is not revealed in the same way as the Holy Spirit in the New Testament. Revelation proceeds from Scripture, whereby the Holy Spirit is revealed as the Third Person in the Trinity in the New Testament. This does not imply, however, that hardly anything or nothing can be deduced about the Holy Spirit in the Old Testament. It is, however, important to reread those sections dealing with the Spirit within the context of both the Old Testament and the specific book in which it occurs. Links can be drawn from the unity of Scripture to the New Testament and the present circumstances. The Spirit in the Old Testament does have implications for pneumatology, especially with regard to the total renewal by the Spirit. In the New Testament, a new meaning is assigned to this when the Holy Spirit brings renewal in Christ.

Kim makes an important contribution to pneumatology and mission, on which some agree and other disagree.[13] She opines that one must understand the variety of supernatural entities and spirits in the world that are viewed as realities or as metaphors of socio-economic powers. She wants to warn against fully rejecting the convictions of other traditions. According to her, tolerance, approached from the principle of hospitality, can lead to a broader understanding of the spiritual world and the work of the Holy Spirit. The spirits will, however, have to be approached from the Spirit of Christ, but, according to her, one should not reject this. One must be prepared to approach the reality of the spiritual world together. According to Kim, others with their own approaches within the Christian conviction

---

11. Kaiser, "Holy Spirit in the Old Testament," 315.
12. Dumbrell, "Spirit and Kingdom," 10.
13. Kim, "The Holy Spirit in the World," 189.

do not essentially have to be included, but there must be space for each other. One must live with from the Spirit of Christ.

Kim criticizes Bosch, because she opines that his pneumatology is too Christ-centered and church-bound.[14] According to her, Bosch lacks understanding of the true postmodern approach to the Spirit. She thus believes that one should rather understand feministic and ecological approaches. One will also have to acknowledge other spirits in order to understand that this is not only about the Spirit of mission but also about the mission of the Spirit.

It must be pointed out that the Holy Spirit as Spirit of Christ differs radically from the spirits of other religions. The close bond between Christ and the Holy Spirit will be pointed out throughout. That unique bond also means that the Holy Spirit is totally different from the other spirits. Mission will have to emphasize this.

In this respect, the present emphasis on "lived religion" must be criticized. Hermans points out that this includes a broader meaning of religiosity.[15] The Christian should not impose his/her understanding on others. She/he should rather be aware of the possibility of experiencing salvation in various ways of being. Accordingly, healthy religiosity means that one should acknowledge these possibilities. Ganzevoort and Roeland have a broad understanding of "lived religion" and opine that the concept of "religion" should be understood in broad terms and that the person himself/herself should determine it. It will be shown throughout that the Holy Spirit emphasizes the fact that Jesus is LORD.[16]

THE HOLY SPIRIT AS MEDIATOR

Exegetic approach

John 16:7–13 is the most essential text on the Holy Spirit and mission. It emphasizes Jesus himself, the Holy Spirit, the Father, and the disciples. Its inter-Trinitarian significance is that the Spirit glorifies Jesus in his continuous work and that the Father receives the Son as the one who effects redemption. The Father and the Son also have that wonderful relationship that is confirmed by the Spirit. For this reason, the Spirit will convey whatever he

14. Kim, "Post-Modern Mission," 177.
15. Hermans, "Lived Spirituality and Lived Religion," 122.
16. Ganzevoort and Roeland, "Lived Religion," 96.

receives from Christ. The concept of "truth" plays a decisive role. The Spirit is the Spirit of truth and will guide in the whole truth. As such, the Spirit is linked to the living truth of the living Christ. For this reason, the Spirit will also glorify Christ. This expresses the close relationship between Christ and the Spirit. The Paraclete is the Spirit of truth and glorifies Christ who is the way, the truth, and the life (John 14:6). The Paraclete will be sent to the Father, and this corresponds with the Son being sent. The Paraclete will speak for Jesus.[17] Together with the disciples, the Paraclete testifies that Jesus is the Light and Truth. Beasley-Murray confirms this:

> The witness of the Spirit, conjoined with that of the disciples, is to bring to light the truth of the revelation of Jesus in his word and deed, and death and resurrection; it takes place with and through the witness of the disciples to Jesus in the Gospel. Clearly this witness of the Paraclete is not a phenomenon apart from that of the disciples, but inseparably associated with it.[18]

According to Brown, the Gospel of John has a clear link with the other Gospels, although John deals with issues in a unique way.[19] In John, ecclesiology, the sacraments, eschatology, and wisdom have a specific, unique slant. He expresses his understanding of these matters in a unique way. In light of the persecution of Christians, the role of the Paraclete, the Holy Spirit, is of great importance. He will highlight the sins of the world.[20] Barrett also opines that, in his Gospel, John emphasizes the history of Jesus, with the intention of confirming belief in Jesus.[21] This is written down so that people can come to faith. Barrett writes: "It is of fundamental importance to John that Jesus did in fact live and die and rise from the dead; but he uses the material in his Gospel so that men may recognize their relation to God in Jesus, rather than to convey interesting information about him."[22]

DeSilva emphasizes that the Gospel of John especially shows the message from above and gives a specific spiritual character to the Gospel.[23] He wants to reinforce the message that Jesus is LORD.[24] The Holy Spirit is

---

17. Beasley-Murray, *John*, 272.
18. Beasley-Murray, *John*, 272.
19. Brown, *Virginal Conception and Bodily Resurrection of Jesus*, cxxvi.
20. Brown, *Virginal Conception and Bodily Resurrection of Jesus*, 698.
21. Barrett, *John*, 5.
22. Barrett, *John*, 5.
23. DeSilva, *New Testament*, 391.
24. DeSilva, *New Testament*, 403.

THE HOLY SPIRIT

not only the one who effects rebirth through Jesus himself, but he is also the one who glorifies Jesus and labels him as Righteous.[25] Joubert refers to how John uses metaphors to express the significance of the Holy Spirit as Paraclete.[26] He uses the metaphors of dove, water, and wind. As far as the dove is concerned, Joubert points out that characteristics such as gentleness, purity, innocence, grace, tenderness, peace, and tranquility are referred to as metaphorical characteristics of the Paraclete.[27] The fruit of the Spirit is associated with the metaphor of the dove. As far as the metaphors of water and wind are concerned, Joubert shows that these emphasize the specific characteristics of the Paraclete.[28] In this regard, the reference to Joel is also of interest. Like the wind, the working of the Spirit is also discernible. The wind as well as God's sovereign work were totally unpredictable in ancient times. The rebirth through the Spirit is also a mystery and independent, like the wind. The Paraclete-Spirit is autonomous, and one can not pretend to understand it.[29] There is thus a new beginning when the Spirit brings renewal through rebirth.

Keener explains John 16:7–13:

> The Paraclete is better for them than Jesus in the flesh would have been (16:7) because he represents Jesus dynamically to the world in each hostile situation. Jesus had also challenged the world concerning sin, righteousness, and judgment, and the prophetic Spirit, proclaiming the same Jesus through his community, would continue the challenge. This continuity between the two should not be understood as identity, as in the docetic reading of John, nor even to imply that the Spirit cannot bring new teachings; the Spirit will say some new things (16:12–13) but in continuity with Jesus' revelation. But it does mean that Jesus himself is present in the Spirit, though only those in his community recognize his presence.[30]

Mission can only be understood by emphasizing the triune work of the Holy Spirit: to convict of sin, justice, and judgment. Haenchen puts this as follows: "These verses speak in a curious way of what the spirit has to do:

---

25. DeSilva, *New Testament*, 433.
26. Joubert, "Johannine Metaphors/Symbols," 18.
27. Joubert, "Johannine Metaphors/Symbols," 18.
28. Joubert, "Johannine Metaphors/Symbols," 18–20.
29. Joubert, "Johannine Metaphors/Symbols," 98.
30. Keener, *John*, 1.1029–30.

the spirit is to convince the world of its sin, namely, that it does not believe in Jesus; of the righteousness of Jesus, namely, that he goes to the Father and so is recognized as justified by the highest authority; and of the judgment that has already been executed over the ruler of this world."[31]

The conviction of sin is essential in mission. Sin is simply not to believe in Christ. It is thus incredibly important for mission to call people to faith in Jesus Christ. Of course, only the Holy Spirit can do this. Inevitably, sin is also broadly worked out in the remainder of Scripture, but, in this instance, it is expressly pointed out. In addition, it is obvious that the justice of Jesus must be emphasized, because law is on his side. Finally, mission must proclaim Jesus Christ's victory over Satan. This wonderful victory was achieved in Jesus Christ.

It is to the good that Jesus is leaving, because he sends the mediator, the Holy Spirit, to his disciples. The Holy Spirit will truly come to the disciples, whose lives emphasize the wonder of God's grace. The disciples will know that there is an advocate, a mediator for them, who also acts on their behalf. A few matters need further attention.

> And when he comes, he will convict the world of its sin, and of God's righteousness, and of the coming judgment. (John 16:8)

The Holy Spirit and the sin of the world

> The world is guilty of sin, because they do not believe in me. (John 16:9)

The Holy Spirit reveals sin. The severity of sin is made public. The Spirit links to Jesus and convinces and creates hope and new life in him. Herod, Pilate, the Jewish leadership, and his own people reject Jesus Christ.

The Holy Spirit will show that the world is guilty of sin. Barrett summarizes the proclamation of the Holy Spirit in this regard as follows:

> The world . . . believes that Jesus was a sinner, justly punished by crucifixion; it believes on the other hand that its own righteousness is all that can be required, and it believes that in these opinions it has rightly judged Jesus and itself, and that its judgment will receive divine confirmation. It is however the work of the Spirit to rectify these wrong notions, and to show that sin consists in the rejection of Jesus, that the only acceptable righteousness is that of

---

31. Haenchen, *John*, 144.

Jesus, since he alone has been exalted to the Father's right hand, and that it is not Jesus but the prince of this world who has been judged.[32]

It is extremely important to emphasize that one must highlight the reality of sin. The emphasis is on the sin of the world. It is obvious that the Holy Spirit will reveal the sin of the world. What sin will the Holy Spirit reveal? The world is guilty of sin because it does not believe in Jesus. The Holy Spirit will point out this sin, namely that the people do not believe in Jesus. The Holy Spirit will reveal that there is truly sin that will be made public. The Holy Spirit plays a revealing role.

Morris writes in this regard:

> The basic sin is the sin which puts self at the centre of things and consequently refuses to believe. This is the world's characteristic sin and it received classic expression when God sent His Son into the world and the world refused to believe in Him. The world is guilty, but it requires the Spirit to sheet this home.[33]

Sin against the Holy Spirit is the only sin that can not be forgiven. This indicates that the work of Christ is attributed persistently to the devil (Matt 12:31–32). Keener writes:

> Third, a heart can become so hard against God's evidence that conversion becomes impossible (12:31–32). Jewish teachers acknowledged that deliberate sin against God's law ("sin with a high hand"—cf. Num 15:30–31; Deut 29:18–20; CD 8.8), such as deliberate blasphemy against God, was unforgivable (Jub. 15:34; 1QS 7.15–17, 22–23; p. Hag. 2:1, §9; cf. Heb 6:6); some recognized that atonement could purify even these sins, but only for the genuinely repentant (CD 10.3; Jas 5:19–20; p. Shebu. 1:6, §5; Ruth Rab. 6:4). Even such a sin as Peter's denial of Jesus (26:69–75) does not count in the unforgivable category (28:10–20), however; the context of "blaspheming against the Spirit" here refers specifically to the sin of these Pharisees, who are on the verge of becoming incapable of repentance. The sign of their hardness of heart is their determination to reject any proof for Jesus' divine mission, to the extent that they even attribute God's attestation of Jesus to the devil.[34]

---

32. Barrett, *Second Epistle to the Corinthians*, 407.
33. Morris, *John*, 698.
34. Keener, *Matthew*, 1112–13. See also Luke 12:10; Mark 3:29.

Welker opines that sin against the Holy Spirit fails to appreciate the possibility that God himself can bring total renewal from misery.[35] Those who fail to appreciate that God himself can make the impossible possible also fail to appreciate God himself. Sin against the Holy Spirit occurs when people, for themselves and for others, block the possibility of God's healing, blessing, and reconciliation. According to Welker, sin against the Holy Spirit implies that the Spirit is singled out as an evil spirit. This denies that the Spirit facilitates the fulfilment of the law, namely through justice and peace. Those who commit sin against the Holy Spirit allege that this forgiveness (life, justice, and peace) by the Spirit is evil.

In light of COVID-19, one must ask whether the pandemic implies only the evolution of viruses. There is also the approach of deism, that God acts like a watchmaker in that he created the earth and then withdrew from the further state of affairs. According to this approach, God would no longer be involved in creation. God is involved in the COVID-19 pandemic, and a few remarks are the order of the day. In a time of COVID-19, mission will indeed also have to take sin seriously. One must acknowledge the reality of sin and God's judgment on sin. The call to conversion is also essential in this respect. The Holy Spirit convinces of sin, so that there can be conversion and renewal and people can take refuge in Jesus.

First, the severity of the sin must be fully realized. This does not simply include things that are done, but a way of existence, namely what we are basically. In Christ, we are also redeemed. Does this mean that there is a link between COVID-19 and sin? Of course, the misery of life is due to sin. God's creation was good. God's judgment over the world comes because of sin. God also works towards advancing life in his creation through his Spirit. It is evident that God's good creation is suffering destruction under sin. The consequences of sin are visible in many aspects of life. The horror of sin must be seriously dealt with. Our misery on earth is the result of sin. God's judgment over sin is thus a reality, also in times of COVID-19.

Secondly, the key aspect for mission must be highlighted, namely that the death on the cross of Jesus Christ has defeated and destroyed sin. This is the heart of mission. For this reason, the Holy Spirit convinces of sin so that people can take refuge in Jesus Christ and obtain redemption. Sin is not to believe in him, and life is to embrace his cross and to believe in him. This gives new perspective to COVID-19. One takes refuge, under the circumstances, to Jesus, the Crucified and Risen LORD. The cross stands

---

35. Welker, *God the Spirit*, 218.

opposite sin. For this reason, there is hope. Mission always calls for conversion. There is only hope in this. God's judgment is averted in the cross.

Thirdly, the only hope is to be found in God. The Holy Spirit creates eschatological hope. He opens the new door to the future, where there is more than life on earth. Mission also creates hope for eternity in Jesus Christ through the Holy Spirit. COVID-19 does not have the last word. There is eternally more than this life. Attention must also be paid to this.

The Holy Spirit as the Spirit of Christ who emphasizes his right

> About righteousness, because I am going to the Father, where you can see me no longer (John 16:10)

The Holy Spirit also convinces of righteousness, namely that the law is on Jesus' side. The law of Jesus is so often violated in the world. He will triumph, but we now see the cross in the world. There are no easy answers. Jesus himself cries out from the cross, "My God, my God, why did you abandon me," but the Holy Spirit comes to his aid; he is raised from the dead. In this world, we see the cross as well as the promise of eternal life. Jesus was judged not guilty. The Holy Spirit will reveal this injustice. Brown confirms this clearly: "The second element (vs. 10) in the Paraclete's forensic activity is to prove the world wrong about justice by showing that Jesus, whom it adjudged guilty, was really innocent and just."[36]

This emphasizes the principle of the law of Jesus, which is extremely important. The law is on his side, and he reveals it. This principle of law also reveals the people for who they are but also for God for who he is. He was judged, but he was saved to walk the road to the cross, on which he confirmed that the law is on his side.

It is important to emphasize the Holy Spirit's special relationship with Jesus Christ. Reformed theology treated the relationship between Christ and the Spirit very seriously. For example, Hyde points to the intimate relationship between the Spirit and Christ.[37] Gaffin explains that the gift of the Spirit is closely linked with Christ.[38] God's law, however, is also broad and includes various aspects. When the law is on Jesus' side, it also includes his

---

36. Brown, *John*, 712.
37. Hyde, "Holy Spirit in the Heidelberg Catechism," 237.
38. Gaffin, "Holy Spirit," 58–78.

involvement in people's distress. His law is indeed the law of his love for people.

The Holy Spirit and judgment

> Judgment has come, because the ruler of this world has already been judged. (John 16:11)

The last aspect is that judgment has already come because the law is on Jesus' side and he is going to his Father. Satan who brings destruction in the world has already been judged and rejected. This emphasizes the holiness of redemption in Jesus Christ.

It appears that the ruler of the world has won. Job would also have experienced this. But the Holy Spirit ensures that judgment has already come. Satan was judged. There are various questions on the aspect of evil spirits. There are few indications of evil spirits in the Old Testament. The New Testament, especially the Synoptic Gospels, abound in indications of evil spirits. Jesus drives the evil spirits out and heals a few of them. Van Rensburg shows that there is no doubt that there are evil spirits.[39] Satan is also a reality. One should adhere to a few aspects. On the basis of a reformed epistemology, Van Heerden shows that it is confessed that Satan has been defeated; that the faithful remains standing only in belief from the link with God against the attacks of the evil powers, not out of his/her own will; that illness does not always come from evil; that demonic influence is not hereditary, and that Christians can not be possessed by the devil. Van Rensburg opines that there are indications that the believer can somehow be "bound."[40] In Luke 13:10–17, we hear of a woman who was bound by Satan, according to Jesus. Paul, in 2 Corinthians 12:1–10, is beaten by Satan's angel. Van Rensburg opines, however, that the phrase "attacks by evil" can solve these differences.[41] Van Rensburg points out that helping those tormented by the occult includes issues such as *katartizein* (recovery, elevation), *oikodomein* (building up), *sterizein* (strenghtening) and *parakalein/nouthetein* (addressing or warning).[42] Based on a covenant model, with the acknowledgment of redemption in Jesus Christ, salvation

---

39. Van Rensburg, *Occult Debate*, 8–19.
40. Van Rensburg, *Occult Debate*, 25–29.
41. Van Rensburg, *Occult Debate*, 37.
42. Van Rensburg, *Occult Debate*, 81–90.

is possible. This is also done by means of a pneumatology model. The Holy Spirit's work and blessing is essential for the redemption from evil spirits. Praying is crucial. The Holy Spirit empowers the pastor in his ministry to help the tormented person. Acceptance of the Holy Spirit's work is also essential.[43]

It is also important to consider the Holy Spirit and violence. Does the Holy Spirit equip people to commit violence? How must one understand sections on violence in the Old Testament? There are various ways of dealing with war and violence in the Old Testament. Tate provides a detailed overview of the various ways in which theologians approach violence in the Old Testament.[44]

First, in Marcion's approach, the "bellicose God" of the Old Testament is not accepted, only the God of love, as suggested in some parts of the New Testament.

The second approach is to spiritualize violence and war by reinterpreting texts on violence and war to mean spiritual war and not physical violence.

The third is a linguistic approach, implying that God as soldier anthromorph should not be understood literally.

The fourth is to emphasize Israel, thus indicating people who must serve God as priests and a holy nation (Ps 147:10–11). Israel is the ideal proffered by God. Rather than the soldier, the ideal person is like Job (Job 29:15–17). Israel's vision is one of peace (Isa 2:4).

Tate also believes that it is not easy to move from war and violence in the Old Testament to contemporary war.[45] This can only be done through humility. Often, God achieves his aim through war. According to Tate, it is impossible to lay down absolute principles. God also achieves his aim in strange ways.[46]

One can indeed agree with Tate. War and violence in the Old Testament can not simply be explained away or spiritualized. They must be interpreted anew. Text must be compared with text. The entire canon must be considered. Despite this, an utterly final last decision for violence can be taken when the Holy Spirit maintains the law of God. The Holy Spirit is

---

43. Van Rensburg, *Occult Debate*, 92–93.
44. Tate, "War and Peacemaking in the Old Testament," 587–94.
45. Tate, "War and Peacemaking in the Old Testament," 594.
46. Tate, "War and Peacemaking in the Old Testament," 594.

not only the Spirit that heals but also the Spirit that carries God's judgment into effect.

This interpretation is also important in understanding violence and war in the Old Testament. This creates the possibility of addressing it as God's intervention to oppose chaos and sin in the totally corrupt world. The Holy Spirit wants to bring this redemption to us.

Sutton and Human address the issues of honor and disgrace in military action. Honor is associated with saving people, also in war.[47] Disgrace is when people are taken prisoner. Sutton also points to recovery after war.[48] Often, according to him, the Psalms point to justified violence. One must, however, guard against accepting violence when the poor and the oppressed are being abused. The authorities carry God's sword and can use violence only under extreme circumstances. There may be opposition under the guidance of the Holy Spirit only when all other possibilities are depleted by a totally corrupt authority. It must be confirmed that the Holy Spirit as Spirit of Christ, the Sovereign of Peace, reveals the horrors of violence and war and calls for peace. There can be no doubt that God, through the Holy Spirit in the individual's heart and in the community, wants to bring peace. The Holy Spirit confirms Christ's work to bring peace in his kingdom. This peace is not the world's peace, but God's peace, which is beyond our comprehension. In order to maintain the law of God, a final way out could be to use violence or go into war, but then always in total brokenness, with minimum action, and in defense.

Van de Beek has a pacifist approach.[49] After the cross, one can no longer reason on the basis of violence. Jesus bears all the misery of the world on the cross. Besides, God himself bears the misery. He opines that all violence must be renounced, especially in light of the pre-Constantine fathers' approach to war and violence. He believes that the action in the wars in Israel can not be applied to the action of contemporary governments.

It is true that Jesus bears the world's misery and that we must always view God's judgment in light of the cross. References in the Old Testament to violence and war may not be conveyed directly to contemporary circumstances. The cross on Golgotha is decisive. God's judgment, however, often calls for fair resistance. One can not possibly reject all self-defense. Augustine, other post-Constantine fathers, and Reformers realized this.

47. Sutton and Human, "Imagery of the Head," 391–410.
48. Sutton, "Clothing Imagery," 336.
49. Van de Beek, *God Lééft*, 77–99.

In deeply repenting the misery of the world, violence must often be dealt with violence. A community of peace is often the result of action by those who sacrifice their life in order to resist greater violence with violence. The community can not enjoy the benefit thereof without acknowledging them. Van de Beek's point of view pleads for deep thought and recognition. One can only differ with him with great hesitation.

God's judgment is also achieved when he calls people to account. He is the overabundant fountain of all good, but he also maintains the law. For this reason, one can not allege that God does not judge. God's law is maintained when God judges. Its culmination is found in the death of Jesus on the cross, where he, for the sake of many, gives his life in order to bring salvation. As the bringer of salvation, Jesus gives himself over so that he can be made sin, in order to bring salvation for many, as clearly expressed in 2 Corinthians 5:19–21.

The Holy Spirit will lead in truth

> When the Spirit of truth comes, he will guide you into all the truth, for he will not speak on his own authority, but whatever he hears he will speak, and he will declare to you the things that are to come. (John 16:13)

The Holy Spirit and Christ are One as they are One with the Father. Pilate asks Jesus, "What is the truth?" (John 18:38). The Holy Spirit answers that Jesus is the truth. He will guide into truth. The Holy Spirit will proclaim what is to come, namely the cross, the resurrection, and the ascension of Jesus. The Holy Spirit is also the Spirit of Peace.

This all renews salvation in Christ. The Spirit is also called the Spirit of the truth, because he will guide into the whole truth. This is not a general truth that will be confirmed; it is a truth that deeply confirms that Jesus is the way, the truth, and the life, as confessed in John 14:6. The Holy Spirit confirms this, and he will guide the disciples into the whole truth, because what he says will not come from him; it is simply what he hears.

Some opine that this is a prophetic statement about future events in the world in general and that those future events will be revealed. This emphasizes that these are the things that lie ahead for Jesus. This instruction is given prior to his crucifixion. The things that will happen in the crucifixion will be revealed, and the Holy Spirit will emphasize the significance of the crucifixion. He will announce this truth by announcing the things that will come. He will honor Jesus because he will announce to the disciples what he received from him. They will understand Christ's instruction and his glory. The wonder of his glory will, in that respect, be highlighted, and the glory of Christ will be emphasized anew, finally, because all that belongs to the Father also belongs to Jesus. This implies the Trinity. The inter-Trinitarian aspect of salvation in Christ is emphasized in a unique way, because it involves the Father, the Son and the Holy Spirit.

The Holy Spirit glorifies Jesus Christ

> He will glorify me, because he will take from what is mine and declare it to you. (John 16:14)

Morris writes: "The work of the Spirit is Christocentric. He will draw attention not to himself but to Christ. He will glorify Christ. It is the things of Christ that he takes and declares, i.e., his ministry is built upon and is the necessary sequel to that of Christ."[50]

The Holy Spirit and Jesus Christ are closely linked to each other. He is from the Father and the Son. He will announce what he receives. Jonker emphasizes that, when God reveals himself in Christ, the work of the Holy Spirit is also visible and that an acknowledgment of the divinity of Christ also emphasizes anew the wonder of the divinity of the Holy Spirit.[51] The Holy Spirit is the end-of-time gift of God who is very closely linked to Christ and comes from the Father and from the Son and does the wonders of the work of the Son. This is never about the Spirit in personal terms, but about the unity of God that is never threatened by the distinction between the Father, the Son, and the Holy Spirit. The Spirit remains the Spirit of the Father and the Son. It must be distinguished from the Father and the Son and is never an impersonal power. It must be confessed that the Spirit is not distinguished to such an extent that we fall into Trinitarianism when there is no unity between Father, Son, and Holy Spirit. The relationship between Christ and the Spirit is important. The Holy Spirit is poured out after Christ's suffering and ascension, and the Holy Spirit gains new significance in a special way.[52] He acts in a very unique way. Often, in the New Testament, it appears that Christ and the Spirit are identified with each

---

50. Morris, *John*, 701.
51. Jonker, *Die Gees van Christus*, 102–05.
52. Jonker, *Die Gees van Christus*, 129.

other, but various texts point out the different aspects of Christ and the Spirit, although the Holy Spirit is acknowledged as the true Spirit of Christ. Brown explains that the Holy Spirit in truth makes known the Father's will in and through Jesus Christ.[53]

Thus, we see the wonder of the Spirit of Christ. He connects us to Jesus. There is hope in the cross of Jesus and the cross of the world.

---

53. Brown, *John*, 716.

The Holy Spirit as the Spirit of Revelation, the Spirit of Life, and the Cosmological Work of the Spirit

REVELATION

It must first be acknowledged that the Holy Spirit always bears and announces revelation. There is evidence that Scripture is inspired by God. The Holy Spirit facilitates this as he works in people's hearts. The Holy Spirit proclaims the word of God to the world in a very unique way.

What is the content of the revelation of the word of God in the world?

There are a number of ways to answer what the Holy Spirit does in realizing the revelation of the word of God, Scripture. One will have to clearly acknowledge that the Spirit uses writers who must maintain their own personalities and writing style. The Holy Spirit is the Spirit of Christ who does the wonder to link Christ and gives grace to really know Christ. The Holy Spirit facilitates our knowledge of Jesus Christ.

Jonker strongly emphasizes that one should not undervalue the relationship between the Spirit and the Bible.[1] The Holy Spirit does not work separately from Scripture. Should he do so, as happened among some of the Pentecostal movements, the relationship between the Spirit and Scripture becomes a problem.[2] Jonker points out that there is indeed a wrong view of the Holy Spirit and that the link between Christ and the Spirit and between Christ and the word is broken. It is extremely important to understand the Holy Spirit and the relationship between the Spirit and Christ in terms of the emphasis of Scripture. As far as the gift of the Spirit is concerned,

1. Jonker, *Die Gees van Christus*, 210.
2. Jonker, *Die Gees van Christus*, 212.

Jonker indicates that the so-called rejection of all gifts by some Protestants is not tenable because Scripture facilitates gifts. He also points to the danger of separating the Holy Spirit and the gifts from Christ and the word. This ultimately results in the gifts becoming too important. Victory over sin must be emphasized.[3] Victory is in the power of God.

There are also references to the way in which Welker approaches revelation, by taking into account the historical circumstances. Van der Westhuizen explains Welker's approach well:

> In order to appreciate the historical and the cultural weight of the biblical traditions it is indicative that the differentiated settings in life and these traditions' influence on the most diverse settings in life are apprehended . . . Welker critically emphasizes, however, that without the further development of the "mystery of Christ and the Holy Spirit," what is meant with "inspiration" will remain impervious and subject to misuse. He therefore answers the question as to the "inspiration" of the biblical traditions on the basis of an articulated theology of the Spirit.[4]

THE COSMOLOGICAL WORK OF THE SPIRIT

Introduction

The issue of the working of the Holy Spirit is immediately evident. Does the Spirit work in the church or beyond the church and in the world? Welker and Van de Beek have different opinions. Jonker and Heyns also acknowledge the cosmological work of the Holy Spirit. Vos emphasizes the eschatological implications of the person and work of the Holy Spirit. Van de Beek is critical of the cosmological work of the Spirit. Initially, he was positive about it. Due to the spirit/theology of the time and present pneumatology, he wants to overemphasize the Spirit's work in the church and sacraments.

Jonker

Jonker acknowledges the cosmological work of the Spirit from the fact that the reformatory principle confirms this.[5] Jonker points to the work of the

---

3. Jonker, *Die Gees van Christus*, 241.
4. Van der Westhuizen, "Michael Welker's Theological Hermeneutics," 613.
5. Jonker, *Die Gees van Christus*, 248.

Holy Spirit and the danger of salvation individualism. He points out that problems arise when the work of the Holy Spirit acquires revolutionary and political implications.[6] The theology of liberation asks the Holy Spirit for a revolutionary task. What is Jonker's answer to this? He opines that one can accept the cosmological work of the Holy Spirit. The Holy Spirit works widely and impressively in creation. One should also acknowledge the specific work of the Holy Spirit.[7] Understanding the work of the Holy Spirit in reality is thus not so much the difference between nature and grace, but between sin and grace. Reformed theology has always recognized that God also works widely. Sin suppresses God's truth, wonder, and significance. That is the reason why the Holy Spirit works in a renewed way. One must acknowledge the danger of individualism. Christianity does not want to underestimate earthly life, but always guards against dualism. On the other hand, Jonker points out that the Holy Spirit binds us to Christ and that we must learn to know Christ through the work of the Holy Spirit. The relationship between Christ and the Sprit, as well as the role of the Paraclete in John 14–16, are extremely important.[8]

Van de Beek and Welker

Van de Beek and Welker have different views. Van de Beek views the Holy Spirit as the Spirit of Christ that works in the church and from there in creation.[9] The Spirit of Christ renews and brings change in the church. The Spirit of Christ also renews the world through the church, but the Spirit is not a cosmological spirit that works without Christ and the church in the world. This world fell into sin and was removed from God. The Spirit works in the world through the church, and the church establishes the new community of God. The church is thus very important. Van de Beek mentions the salvation-bringing work of the Spirit in the church, and the unity of the church is thus as important. There is absolute unity in God, and one must acknowledge the unity of the church. God is One, but the church must also be one, because we believe in God. The Spirit is present in the

---

6. Jonker, *Die Gees van Christus*, 256.
7. Jonker, *Die Gees van Christus*, 265.
8. Jonker, *Die Gees van Christus*, 265–70.
9. Van de Beek, *Lichaam en Geest van Christus*, 430–31.

sacraments, which reveal the intimate relationship between Christ and the Holy Spirit.[10]

Van de Beek strongly emphasizes two aspects.[11] First, the Holy Spirit is very closely linked to Christ. The Holy Spirit and the church can not be viewed as separate entities. The church is most deeply bound to both the sacraments and preaching. Word and sacrament are interdependent. Christ is present in the sacrament. He thus detaches himself from the idea that the Spirit merely works in the cosmos, with his criticism of the destructive aspects of reality, because the Spirit is linked to Christ in the *new* creation. Secondly, he rejects the idea that the Spirit represents the general good. Criticism is levelled against Welker's approach that the church is a resistance movement against power structures and thus generalizes the believers.

By contrast, Welker opines that the Holy Spirit works generally in the world. Conradie points out that Van der Westhuizen describes Welker's pneumatology as follows:

> The focus is therefore on "the actions of the living God" in terms of creation, maintenance and salvation, that is, the economic Trinity. Welker's "realistic" theology takes experiences of the Spirit as a point of departure, also within the biblical roots of the subsequent Christian tradition. Such experiences are then interpreted through a Pneumatological and indeed a Trinitarian lens. The Spirit forms a community, that is, a communion with the crucified and risen Jesus Christ.[12]

The Holy Spirit renews the world, ultimately resulting in the new heaven and the new earth. The renewed world becomes a totally new world. The Holy Spirit renews in a unique and specific manner because the Holy Spirit creates this renewal. The Holy Spirit is both the Spirit of Christ and the Spirit that works in places of which people are not necessarily aware. Welker points to continuity because, according to him, the Spirit works anew in a new world. The question is whether Van de Beek and Welker are so radically opposed. Welker views the Spirit as the Spirit of Christ, and for that reason also the Spirit determines the church and is bound in word and sacrament. The Spirit works in and through the sacrament. For Welker, the Spirit is not restricted to this. The Spirit is also specific in his work

---

10. Van de Beek, *Lichaam en Geest van Christus*, 430–31.
11. Van de Beek, *Lichaam en Geest van Christus*, 424–36.
12. Conradie, "Triune God," 1–11.

and must, according to Welker, not be generalized, even if the Spirit effects righteousness, peace, and salvation.

Heyns

Heyns refers to two aspects of the work of the Holy Spirit. First, the cosmological work of the Holy Spirit,[13] which means that the Spirit together with the Father and the Son not only maintain creation but also, based on general grace and revelation, participate in the salvation and confirmation of God's graceful work, even among those who do not believe.

Heyns refers to the work of the Spirit in Genesis 1:2 who, as *ruach Elohim*, sways over the shapeless, unordered, primitive world that is then ultimately ordered, prepared, and repaired. All life is the work of the Holy Spirit. God also claims the sinful world for himself, and the world can not say that they have no interest in what God does through the Holy Spirit. God claims the sinful world, and the Holy Spirit also has a part therein. Heyns further emphasizes that the Holy Spirit does and continues to do his work and cosmological work out of grace.[14] This does not mean, however, that people are automatically saved or guided into glory. The cosmological work of the Holy Spirit can also cause the revelation of God in nature, history, and man's life. God reveals himself in that sense to those who are not necessarily in Christ (Rom 1:20; Ps 8:3; 2 Sam 23:2). Heyns finds the soteriological work of the Holy Spirit important.[15] The Holy Spirit's cosmological work occurs on the level of natural life so as to confirm it and to ensure that it does not totally go to ruin. The saving work of the Holy Spirit is a unique and specific work associated with predestination. The Father, the Son, and the Holy Spirit collaborate in the predestination of people in order to incorporate them in the covenant. As bridge-builder in the covenant of grace, the Holy Spirit incorporates man in Christ's salvation.[16]

In the incarnation of the Word, the Holy Spirit effects the historical realization of the covenant for the coming of Christ to the world. It is a unique soteriological work of the Holy Spirit that redemption takes place in Christ. The Holy Spirit is also active in writing the word. In this instance, it is very clear that one can not ignore the wonder of the Holy Spirit in the

13. Heyns, *Dogmatiek*, 296.
14. Heyns, *Dogmatiek*, 297.
15. Heyns, *Dogmatiek*, 298.
16. Heyns, *Dogmatiek*, 299.

soteriological work in the inspiration of the Bible in this unique specific way.

Dingemans

Dingemans wants almost the whole of theology to be absorbed in pneumatology.[17] For him, God is Spirit, and God must be known as Spirit. Although he does not use the concept of the cosmological work of the Holy Spirit, he is of the opinion that *pneuma* manifests in various ways, and this includes the Creator. God is then understood as a power or *pneuma* that stands above and behind reality and that personifies him in Jesus. According to Dingemans, God is not the Almighty, but he is the voice that calls for the future.[18]

Jesus is full of the Spirit even after his death.[19] As Spirit, he continuously exerts influence on the world.[20] The one God manifests in three ways, but God is one *pneuma* that works in different ways. The *pneuma* is the power (*energeia*) of God that goes out into the entire world.[21] Dingemans especially opines that the *pneuma* also works in other nations and cultures.[22] It goes without saying that God works in all cultures and religions, but the answer differs. The Spirit is also the Creator of heaven and earth (Gen 1:1–2).[23]

Van de Beek's criticism against Welker and Dingemans is, however, of great importance. The Spirit can not be separated from the personal God in his unity. The church, as church of Christ, is renewed by the Spirit of Christ, with a view to new creation. The community of faith thereby has a totally new meaning. Mission is then understood anew, because, through the Spirit and in the church, people are bound to Christ anew. There is the possibility of new life and new future in Christ through the Spirit. According to Heyns, there must be room for the Spirit that maintains the world so that it does not fall into total ruin.

---

17. Dingemans, *Pneumatologie*, 15.
18. Dingemans, *Pneumatologie*, 135–36.
19. Dingemans, *Pneumatologie*, 140.
20. Dingemans, *Pneumatologie*, 141.
21. Dingemans, *Pneumatologie*, 143.
22. Dingemans, *Pneumatologie*, 156.
23. Dingemans, *Pneumatologie*, 160.

Kärkkäinen

Kärkkäinen establishes his premises in his pneumatology as follows.[24] First, he wants to describe the present world with all its different aspects in order to practice a theology that significantly answers its challenges. He approaches pneumatology from the perspective of answering in detail the questions of the contextual world around him. The premise is thus very important for him, because he wants to formulate an answer and intensively interact with the present world around him. In addition, he wants to approach pneumatology from a deep Christian conviction in order to discuss other convictions and other religious points of view in detail. Kärkkäinen states his point of view as follows:

> Systematic/constructive theology is an integrative discipline that continuously searches for a coherent, balanced understanding of Christian truth and faith in light of Christian tradition (biblical and historical) and in the context of historical and contemporary thought, cultures and living faiths. It aims at a coherent, inclusive, dialogical and hospitable vision.[25]

This is the starting point of Kärkkäinen's approach to his systematic theology, but from this perspective he also wants to establish certain matters concerning the Holy Spirit.

Kärkkäinen also finds the work of the Holy Spirit in art and relaxation, because the Holy Spirit brings freedom on various levels.[26] He again discusses this with other theologies and approaches. Kärkkäinen's emphasis on the Holy Spirit in the Trinitarian approach is very important. It differs from the classical model in that he would rather place more emphasis on the Spirit in relation to others.

One will have to acknowledge Van de Beek's specific contribution that the Trinitarian unity shows the Spirit's specific work in Christ. This aspect is very important for Van de Beek. It is a non-negotiable significance that the Spirit continues with the work of Jesus Christ. The Spirit can not be separated from Christ. For this reason, the Spirit is not a general spirit of unity and good disposition, but rather a Spirit that works in Christ in a renewing manner through the church.

---

24. Kärkkäinen, *Spirit and Salvation*, 2–10.
25. Kärkkäinen, *Spirit and Salvation*, 2.
26. Kärkkäinen, *Spirit and Salvation*, 179–85.

Vos

Vos explains the implications of the relationship between Christ and the Holy Spirit for pneumatology. He opines that the whole of theology is associated with the relationship between Christ and the Holy Spirit. He shows how the Old Testament attaches a specific meaning to the concept of "Spirit," which does not necessarily imply the fullness of the Holy Spirit. Specific lines can be drawn from the Old Testament to the New Testament. In the latter, the great line is the relationship between Christ and the Holy Spirit. In the Old Testament, the Spirit is Creator and Maintainer, and this should not be directly linked with the Holy Spirit. In the New Testament, the relationship is bound to Christ in a special sense. That is the reason why the Spirit is called the Spirit of Christ, as expressly mentioned by Paul.

Vos shows how the Spirit has special implications for eschatology.[27] This must also be understood as significant of the Pentecost events. The Pentecost celebration is the seed in the bedding, where the Holy Spirit is emphasized as wonder in the New Testament. For this reason, he also has eschatological meaning, as highlighted in the Pentecost events.

Vos thus describes the relationship between Christ and the Holy Spirit from the Pentecost events, which can only be described in eschatology-salvation historical terms.[28] He points out that the Holy Spirit continues the work of Christ in order to bring it to fullness.[29] In Romans 8:9, the salvation-historical-eschatological unity between Christ and the Holy Spirit is understood in two ways. On the negative side, whoever does not have the Spirit does not belong to Christ. On the positive side, the relationship with the Holy Spirit implies the wonder of a new relationship. The faithful then enters the power sphere of the Holy Spirit, because the Holy Spirit also lives in the faithful.

The meaningful search for the Holy Spirit's own identity remains a theological exercise.[30] According to Vos, it creates Trinitarian room for God within this context. This is worked out in the cosmos, so that it is ready for complete re-creation. The Holy Spirit is also a sign of the future. Vos has a crucial element that emphasizes eschatology, namely that the Holy Spirit

---

27. Vos, *Heilige Gees*, 222.
28. Vos, *Heilige Gees*, 223.
29. Vos, *Heilige Gees*, 225.
30. Vos, *Heilige Gees*, 247.

is also oriented to the future, to re-creation, to renewal, and, as sign of the future, as Paraclete.[31]

The Paraclete will thus emphasize different aspects, such as the future, the glorification of Christ.[32] He will also guide the disciples throughout the world into the whole truth, and the way and the truth will be in Christ. He shows the way of Christ's truth. When the Paraclete leads the person on the path of truth, he experiences a tense relationship with sin and injustice.[33]

Vos mentions that the Holy Spirit represents total legacy, the eschatological legacy, and that the Holy Spirit vouches for the full completion thereof.[34] There is already a kind of realized eschatology of the future; a sign from God announces his future to his children. This is a promise of the fullness to come. For this reason, one is anxiously expecting the future and, with songs of praise, a call to God because of a pledge of future glory.

In addition, the Holy Spirit is the sign of the creature's future, that rebirth will take place. Those who believe in Christ will also be assured of this cosmological-eschatological gift.

Vos opines that the cosmological work of the Spirit can be mentioned, but this is also tied to eschatology. Unlike Welker, this aligns with Van de Beek that the Spirit's work is very closely linked to the church. Vos leaves room for the work of the Spirit in creation. He thus also highlights other perspectives than those of Van de Beek. Reference to the Holy Spirit's cosmological-eschatological gift is a big reward.

Migliore

Migliore points to the fact that there is a new interest in the person and work of the Holy Spirit because the Holy Spirit is not only above and for us but also in our work, and he works within us in a special way.[35] Migliore protests against the depersonalization of the bureaucracy of modern society. There is a desire for deeper faith.[36] He questions the cold objectivity of modern society and ordinary rationality. The ecumenical church also strongly highlights the fact that many ministers, pastors, and church leaders mention a

---

31. Vos, *Heilige Gees*, 247.
32. Vos, *Heilige Gees*, 250.
33. Vos, *Heilige Gees*, 251.
34. Vos, *Heilige Gees*, 255.
35. Migliore, *Faith Seeking Understanding*, 224.
36. Migliore, *Faith Seeking Understanding*, 225.

feeling of emptiness and want to experience a new spiritual life.[37] There is a new understanding of the work of the Holy Spirit in both the Old and the New Testament. Specific aspects of the Holy Spirit must be highlighted. Scripture must form the basis of the work of the Holy Spirit in the history of Israel, in Christ's behavior and service, and in the life of the early church. The believer is thus bound to Christ and finds new life and community in him. This means that the work of the Holy Spirit represents Christ. Christ is brought into contemporary life where he creates a new liberating life. The Holy Spirit brings new freedom. He creates community, *koinonia*, that binds us to Christ and to the other. The promise associated with the work of the Holy Spirit who brings renewal and the charismata given by the Holy Spirit develop the church.

The work of the Holy Spirit corresponds with the wonder of redemption and of the activity of the Spirit in Eternal Life. The Holy Spirit binds us to Christ, pours out the love of God in our hearts, gives us new life, helps us pray, frees us for the love of God and our neighbor, makes us God's people, and calls us to glorify God.[38]

Like the Father and the Son, the Holy Spirit must also be honored and worshipped. The Spirit is the Spirit of the triune God who works in us. The world must thus be approached from the power of the Holy Spirit.[39] The Holy Spirit is from Christ (*filioque*).

The question is whether the Holy Spirit should be described as a woman.[40] In Hebrew, *ruach* is feminine; in Greek, *pneuma* is neutral; and, in Latin, *spiritus* is masculine. Migliore points out that God is more than simply gender and that one should not lapse into this in order to uphold specific opinions that do not glorify the Holy Spirit. In terms of the linguistic aspects, one can not refer to the Holy Spirit as feminine.

Migliore also understands that the Holy Spirit works and acts outside the church. To him, the cosmological work of the Spirit is a complex issue. He refers to past attempts at trying to understand it as general grace or general revelation. He opines, however, that it is essential to talk about the cosmological work of the Holy Spirit because it presumes the freedom

---

37. Migliore, *Faith Seeking Understanding*, 226.
38. Migliore, *Faith Seeking Understanding*, 230.
39. Migliore, *Faith Seeking Understanding*, 232.
40. Migliore, *Faith Seeking Understanding*, 233.

of the Holy Spirit and it highlights the responsibility of the church in the world.[41]

In Christian life, the Holy Spirit works on justification and sanctification.[42]

The cosmological Spirit and the spirit of Africa

There is the danger of viewing Africa's traditional religion as uniform throughout sub-Saharan Africa. Mbiti's attempt at specific uniformity is dismissed.[43] Despite this, there could still be specific similarities.

Van der Walt refers in detail to aspects of Africa's traditional society, by describing the world and the mediating role of the spiritual powers.[44] According to him, the reason for this mediator is that God is viewed as distant and can not be directly approached. The mediators must be the way whereby God can be reached. These spiritual mediators have different characteristics and take the message to the divine being. There are various kinds of spiritual powers, namely divine beings, semi-divine beings, spiritual beings, and ancestors. The latter are very important. One's place is very important in a relationship with the ancestors, because ancestors determine one's well-being and future to a large extent. The ancestors can make specific forms of medicines more powerful, protect people from witch doctors, take away all forms of evil and misery, provide victory in war, and explain all kinds of secrets. The spiritual world is thus real.

Several African theologians try to bridge the border between the Christian gospel and the world of their ancestors. However, according to Van der Walt, one must acknowledge the difference that has deep significance for the existence of spiritual powers. Van der Walt especially emphasizes that there must be an integral biblical world image, a life and world view, and that this is the key to the redevelopment of Africa.

In traditional Africa, there are different ways of referring to spiritual powers. Some emphasize that the *animus* is active and that there are spiritual powers everywhere in nature. Everything has meaning, and spiritual powers live and work there. The ancestors' spirits are especially important. When the ancestors pass away, they do not necessarily turn into nothing;

---

41. Migliore, *Faith Seeking Understanding*, 235.
42. Migliore, *Faith Seeking Understanding*, 239.
43. Mbiti, *Concepts of God*.
44. Van der Walt, *Understanding and Rebuilding Africa*, 72–73.

they can continue to exist and still work in this reality. They are still significant. This means that the spirits work and are present in reality in a very special way. Is the spirit that is acknowledged among specific communities of African traditional groups and the Spirit of Christ similar? Or should one distinguish in detail between the Spirit of Christ who brings renewal in the church and the spirit of Africa that often appears in Africa's traditional religion? Ferdinando explains how criticism has been levelled against the way in which Western Christians reject Africa's traditional religion.[45] Bediako's criticism against the way in which Western missionaries dealt with the identity and culture of Africa is important. Cultural superiority and pride must be rejected, according to Ferdinando.[46] One must acknowledge cultural diversity. He points out that Christian missionaries could simply not accept some aspects of the traditional religion, and that life in Africa was not ideal for both missionaries and the traditional people.[47] Bediako shows that African theology succeeds in moving beyond the ethnocentrism of Western missionaries in order to establish a clear pre-Christian Africa tradition, enabling them to creatively and constructively provide their own answer as variant of Christian faith among their people.[48] Gichaara points out attempts at reconciling traditional Africa and Christianity so that the African culture is fully acknowledged.[49] According to him, various aspects of the cosmology of Africa correspond with Christian cosmology. Jenkins emphasizes that too much attention is paid to one's own interpretation and too little to aspects of society itself.[50] He shows that the traditional communities are also moral communities and that hardly any attention was paid to that. Ngong also shows that the communities in Africa emphasize life and that living religion must take note thereof.[51] In many respects, renewal did not come through the gospel. Kenzo and Martin opine that the postmodern movement makes it possible to view anew the positive in Africa.[52] O'Neill explains that the issue of natural law is important in the

---

45. Ferdinando, "Christian Identity in the African Context," 140–45.
46. Ferdinando, "Christian Identity in the African Context," 140–45.
47. Ferdinando, "Christian Identity in the African Context," 140.
48. Bediako, "African Theology in the 20th Century," 17.
49. Gichaara, "African Liberation Theology," 78.
50. Jenkins, "'Longue Durée' in African History Challenges," 261.
51. Ngong, "Salvation in African Theology," 373.
52. Kenzo and Martin, "Postcolonialism, Postmodernism, and the Future of African Theology," 338.

search for ethics in Africa.[53] Brand warns against demonizing aspects of African religion.[54] Maluleke asks for a coherent African theology that is essential for society in Africa.[55] Munga shows how constructive criticism on African theologies must pave the way for renewal in the theology in Africa.[56] As far as the Holy Spirit is concerned, Macchia points out that churches in Africa involve the earlier meaning of the work of the spirit in the new interpretation of the Holy Spirit's work.[57] In this instance, one must thoroughly distinguish between the spiritual world of Africa and the Spirit of Christ. Maluleke, however, is extremely cautious in mentioning that one must accept a specific hermeneutic approach of the Bible.[58] He differs from Mbiti, who criticized the way in which some African theologians use the Bible to proffer new models thereof. This proffered hermeneutic approach differs from those of theologians described by Maleleke.

With regard to these spiritual powers, one can not accept that this is on the same level. The wonders of the Spirit of Christ work in the church, and, for this reason, mission had to bring a new Spirit to people who supported African traditional religion. A new understanding of how the Spirit works is thus essential. The Spirit works on redemption and renewal, causing a change in man. The Holy Spirit is the Spirit of Christ who works in the church for renewal. When it works in nature and in other aspects of our existence, it is not the Spirit that is linked to magic, witchcraft, and ancestors, but it is the Spirit that works for renewal from Christ, and he must always be associated with Christ. This can not be separated from Christ; Christ himself causes this renewal.

One needs to discuss in detail the Spirit in Africa in order to proclaim the true Spirit of Christ that effects renewal and change so that we can understand the fullness of Christ. The latter can only be understood if, in this world, we link the Spirit of Christ to Christ himself. The spiritual powers of this world are often opposed to, resist, and work against Christ, to some extent, but the Spirit of Christ is the Spirit that brings renewal and change in this world.

---

53. O'Neill, "African Moral Theology," 138.
54. Brand, "Witchcraft and Spirit Beliefs in African Christian Theology," 49.
55. Maluleke, "Identity and Integrity in African Theology," 37.
56. Munga, "Changes in African Theology," 254.
57. Macchia, "African Enacting Theology," 106–09
58. Maluleke, "African Christian Theologies," 14–15.

Approach

Does the Holy Spirit work in creation? From an exegetical perspective, there are many questions as to the application of Genesis 1:1–2 as the Creator spirit and as to whether the cosmological work of the Holy Spirit can be inferred from this. *Ruach Elohim* can also be viewed as the great wind and as the Spirit of God that blows over the unformed reality where God then ultimately creates reality to be respected. There are differences of opinion on this topic. As pointed out earlier, Vos does not link the Spirit in the Old Testament directly to the Holy Spirit.[59] There is no doubt that God is involved in creation. Opinions differ as to how God is involved therein.

From an evolutionary perspective, the question is often raised as to whether these were simply the processes that were sent in motion by the Big Bang. Could one then still speak of God as forming creation and calling all things into being? God's work is, however, evident in the fact that God calls reality to exist. One could then extremely cautiously confess that the Holy Spirit also works cosmologically, which is evident in creation, although this can not be inferred from Genesis 1:1–2. The Holy Spirit's work is always done from Christ. Jesus himself is involved in creation (John 1:1–2). Therefore, because the Spirit and Christ are very closely linked, one could by inference allege that the Spirit also works cosmologically in creation. The cosmological work of the Spirit must always be linked to Jesus Christ. Cosmological work occurs from Christ and from the church. In agreement with Van de Beek, this work must take place through Christ and his church.

That acknowledgment would confirm God's work in Jesus. Mission will have to emphasize that the Spirit is very closely linked to Jesus Christ. This implies that the Holy Spirit as the Spirit of Christ is the person in the Trinity who does not act alone. This means that the Trinity, the Father, the Son, and the Holy Spirit, are in a special unity with each other. The Spirit of Christ glorifies Christ. The Spirit can not be viewed as separate from Christ.

The cosmological work of the Holy Spirit will always have to be viewed in connection with the work of Christ. Where the work of Christ is highlighted, so will the work of the Holy Spirit be highlighted. Where the Holy Spirit glorifies Christ, the work of the Holy Spirit is evident. The Holy Spirit can not be a spirit that tears apart and does not glorify Christ.

The Holy Spirit fully accomplishes the work of Christ. Where the Holy Spirit works, Christ is glorified. The Holy Spirit emphasizes that Christ is

---

59. Vos, *Heilige Gees*, 83–85.

the one from whom and through whom and to whom all things are. He is the way, the truth, and the life. The uniqueness and absolute glorification of Christ can never be undervalued because the Holy Spirit confirms this.

In terms of mission, it is extremely important to ask the question, What is the role of the Holy Spirit in mission? Mission can not only be approached from a Christomonist point of view but also from a Christocentric and pneumatological point of view. The role of the Holy Spirit is extremely important in this respect. The Holy Spirit plays a decisive role in the way in which renewal can take place in society through the church. The Holy Spirit is not only a power or a panentheistic movement that works in the world, but it is also truly the Third Person of the Divine Trinity who must be known as person and be glorified as the person of Christ.

The Implications of the Person and Work of the Holy Spirit

THE SIGNIFICANCE OF the Trinity is very important. The Spirit is indeed the Third Person in the Trinity. Matthew 28:19: "Therefore go and make disciples of all nations, baptizing them in the name of the Father and of the Son and of the Holy Spirit."

Heyns approaches pneumatology from the perspective of the Holy Spirit as a person in the Trinity of God.[1] The Spirit reveals all the characteristics of a person as well as all the traits of true divinity. Father, Son, and Holy Spirit form the Trinity. According to Heyns, the wonder of the Holy Spirit is that God empowers and sends out the Spirit for Christ in a very special way. He explains that the Spirit sends out Christ and that Christ is the one whom the Holy Spirit sends out into the world. This clearly expresses the wonder of the Holy Spirit that descends on and empowers Christ as well as the important aspect that Christ himself sends out the Holy Spirit into the world.

Welker raises the important question as to whether we can still speak of the Holy Spirit as a person.[2] He opines that we can indeed talk about the Spirit as a person within the context of the New Testament, where the personality of the Holy Spirit is associated with the fact that the Holy Spirit himself does not work but that it is the work of Christ and that this relationship between Christ and the Holy Spirit is very important. He does, however, warn against a narrow understanding of the term "person." Although he initially mentions the Holy Spirit as force field, as the public

1. Heyns, *Dogmatiek*, 291.
2. Welker, "The Spirit in Philosophical, Theological and Interdisciplinary Perspectives," 226.

person of Christ, as Christ's sounding board in the world, he works it out later Christologically using the three functions of Christ. The Holy Spirit is not amorphous; his personal character lies in the relationship with God the Creator and the sovereignty of Christ.

Jonker emphasizes that one can not undervalue the divinity of the Holy Spirit.[3] The Holy Spirit and Christ are in a close relationship with each other. He also points out that the Holy Spirit in both the early church and the early theologies was viewed as a person who exists in a special unity with the Father and the Son. He also emphasizes the specific meaning of *filioque* as the special relationship between the Holy Spirit and Christ.

Berkhof mentions the active presence of God.[4] Access to the Spirit comes via God in the present.[5] The Spirit also determines Jesus. Both are the fruit of the other.[6] God works among people through the Spirit. Christ and the Spirit are the poles of the new covenant.[7] Through participation, the Spirit effects the work of Christ in man. Through the Holy Spirit, Jesus' work has meaning.[8] God as one God must be acknowledged in his person.

For Kärkkäinen,[9] the relationship of the Holy Spirit with the other persons of the Trinity is interesting, although he opines that the Holy Spirit often appears to be elusive. Ultimately, he emphasizes the Holy Spirit's divinity. The Holy Spirit is indeed the divine Spirit in the Trinity of the triune "Communion."[10] He emphasizes, to some extent, the *koinonia* in the Trinity and refers to the specific meaningful relationship where God also lives for others.[11] In his approach to *filioque*, Kärkkäinen refers to its special significance and how it must also be accounted for, because the Holy Spirit is in a relationship with Christ.[12] Kärkkäinen strongly emphasizes the fact that one should not deny the divinity of the Holy Spirit.[13]

---

3. Jonker, *Die Gees van Christus*, 102–05.
4. Berkhof, *Christelijk Geloof*, 338.
5. Berkhof, *Christelijk Geloof*, 339.
6. Berkhof, *Christelijk Geloof*, 341.
7. Berkhof, *Christelijk Geloof*, 344.
8. Berkhof, *Christelijk Geloof*, 347.
9. Kärkkäinen, *Spirit and Salvation*, 27.
10. Kärkkäinen, *Spirit and Salvation*, 33.
11. Kärkkäinen, *Spirit and Salvation*, 35.
12. Kärkkäinen, *Spirit and Salvation*, 38.
13. Kärkkäinen, *Spirit and Salvation*, 42.

Dingemans's view of the Trinity includes that he fully supports the unity of God in light of Jewish monotheism.[14] Accordingly, the Spirit influences the world and is the *modus operandi* of God. Unitarianism is rejected. The Spirit has a different *modus operandi* in Jesus himself. Jesus himself and the congregation are oriented to the future.[15] That is why he also starts with the resurrection. It is not a miracle, but the historical Jesus returns as the Risen One in the form of the Spirit. According to Dingemans, the cross is not an act of atonement, but a sign of Jesus' absolute solidarity with people; of God's supreme love and of God's solidarity with those who suffer.[16] It is clear that one can not accept this approach.

One can definitely agree with Jonker, Heyns, and Van de Beek on the special relationship of the Holy Spirit, Christ, and the Father. One should not counteract or undervalue the unity in the Trinity, but rather maintain the distinction between Father, Son, and Holy Spirit. One should not counteract the Holy Spirit's own nature. One should maintain the unit in the Trinity.

APPROACH

Like the Holy Spirit, Revelation 4 also emphasizes the glory of God on his throne. John sees the throne of God and the wonder of the Spirit who glorifies God. He is the one from whom, through whom, and to whom all things are. This glory can only be understood from this special emphasis of Christ. Salvation comes only from Christ himself. This is significant for understanding faith in Jesus Christ and for seeing the wonder of Christ's works. Revelation emphasizes that he is ultimately the slaughtered Lamb who appears before God and stands on the right-hand side of God. Ultimately, he is also worthy of opening the book. The Spirit is sent throughout the world because the Spirit is emphasized as seven spirits. One can not undervalue the Spirit's completeness.

Ultimately, Revelation also emphasizes the completeness of the Holy Spirit, in the salvation in Christ, in the return, and in the new heaven and the new earth. In Revelation 22, Jesus will return when all who belong to him are blessed and he is the bright morning star. Revelation 22:17: "The Spirit and the bride say, 'Come!' And let the one who hears say, 'Come!' Let

---

14. Dingemans, *Pneumatologie*, 513.
15. Dingemans, *Pneumatologie*, 514.
16. Dingemans, *Pneumatologie*, 537.

the one who is thirsty come; and let the one who wishes take the free gift of the water of life."

The Holy Spirit makes it possible for people to come to God and to experience God's salvation. The Holy Spirit invites people to drink the water of life from Jesus Christ. Jesus is the yes and the amen, the Word of God as confirmed by the Holy Spirit.

Ultimately, there is the call: "Amen, come LORD Jesus, come soon" (1 Cor 15:22). The grace of the LORD Jesus is only visible in the expectation that he will come in glory through the working of the Holy Spirit.

This has tremendous implications for mission. Mission can not exist without the work of the Holy Spirit. Mission can not be conveyed into the world without the Holy Spirit completing it. For this reason, the Holy Spirit is unique and works in mission. The Holy Spirit also affects the way in which mission highlights the salvation of God. In this respect, the wonder of the Holy Spirit must be emphasized anew. The Holy Spirit is also the Spirit of reconciliation. One must realize that what Christ does, his reconciliation work, and the call by Paul in 2 Corinthians 5:11, "Reconcile yourself with God," can only take place through the work of the Holy Spirit who brings that aspect of reconciliation, the most profound reconciliation with God fulfilled by the Holy Spirit in Christ. When humans are called to appear before God in their sin, the Holy Spirit fulfils Christ's salvation work in them. Christ's salvation work in the cross is full redemption, but the Holy Spirit then calls on humans to serve Christ and to experience redemption in Christ. The Holy Spirit thus brings total redemption and reconciliation. The latter is from God, as in Romans 5, because God loved the world so much, he loved those who belong to him when they were still sinners. God's love is thus very clear. God addresses and saves the sinner. In 2 Corinthians 5, the Holy Spirit finalizes and works through this redemption in the faith of the believer. This faith is from God's wonderful grace that brings salvation. This redemption ultimately opens the door for man to the glory of God. The unity between Father, Son, and Holy Spirit points to the unity in the personal God who is one being and three persons, Father, Son, and Holy Spirit. This Trinity can not be alienated from each other. One can only know the Father through the Holy Spirit in Christ Jesus. Jesus reveals the Father for us. For this reason, the Old and the New Testament must be read together in the unity of faith that will have to be established for the Christian believer.

THE WORKING OF THE HOLY SPIRIT

Heyns also emphasizes that the Holy Spirit, the Advocate, is unfathomable.[17] The Holy Spirit is also a bridge-builder who continues and confirms the work of Christ in a very specific way. The Holy Spirit is called "the firstborn" because he is the firstborn of the harvest that was reaped that will, in the fullness of time, emphasize the wonder of God's activity.[18] The Holy Spirit is also the guarantee. Heyns emphasizes that the Holy Spirit guarantees, in a very special way, the future and those who belong in the future. He emphasizes the wonder of God's grace in a glorified way.

In terms of the Old Testament, Heyns emphasizes three matters.[19] First, the presence of the Holy Spirit. In the Old Testament, he emphasizes the different texts in which the Holy Spirit acts. Secondly, an ardent longing for the greater work of the Holy Spirit, as with Jeremiah and Ezekiel. Thirdly, the Holy Spirit is also the prophetic prediction of a new future in which the Holy Spirit will accomplish the wonders of God. As noted earlier, one must deal cautiously with the Old Testament's approach to the Spirit. Vos differs from Heyns in this respect.[20] Vos opines that the Spirit in the Old Testament can not directly be linked to the Holy Spirit.

According to Heyns, there is no doubt that, already since the Pentecost events, the Holy Spirit has a very special place in the New Testament.[21] The Holy Spirit's coming was not unexpected, but the Holy Spirit reached the speaker/listener at Pentecost and emphasized the wonderful approach of God's grace.

The Spirit evokes rebirth, as indicated in John 3:5: "Very truly I tell you, no one can enter the kingdom of God unless they are born of water and the Spirit." Keener explains:

> Because Nicodemus missed Jesus' point (3:4), Jesus explains what he means by birth from above, using what is probably an "earthly" analogy (3:12): the rebirth of which Jesus speaks is not physical birth, as Nicodemus supposed (3:4), but a spiritual birth (3:6). By "born from above" (3:3) Jesus probably means born "from God," so 3:5 clarifies this claim with "born from the Spirit." "Born of the Spirit" is clear enough in the context of early Christian teaching

17. Heyns, *Dogmatiek*, 292.
18. Heyns, *Dogmatiek*, 293.
19. Heyns, *Dogmatiek*, 294.
20. Vos, *Die Heilige Gees*, 83–85.
21. Heyns, *Dogmatiek*, 294.

(Gal 4:23, 29; cf. 1 Pet 1:3, 23), but what Jesus means here by "born of water" (and how this helps explain "born from God") is less clear, though it undoubtedly made sense to John's original audience.[22]

True worship comes through the Holy Spirit. John 4:23–24: "Yet a time is coming and has now come when the true worshippers will worship the Father in the Spirit and in truth, for they are the kind of worshippers the Father seeks. God is spirit, and his worshippers must worship in the Spirit and in truth."

The Spirit paves the way to God. Hebrews 9:8: "The Holy Spirit was showing by this that the way into the Most Holy Place had not yet been disclosed as long as the first tabernacle was still functioning." O'Brien emphasizes that the Holy Spirit ushers in the new time:

> The access of the high priest to this realm did not indicate its openness but was the exception that proves the rule. As long as the outer tent had normative status as a sanctuary, it prevented people from seeing, let alone entering, the Most Holy Place. Our author thus shows "the mutual exclusiveness, in theological terms, of the old and new dispensations."[23]

The Spirit is the Spirit that equips and blesses, because the spirit works in people. The way in which the Spirit empowers is not simply to empower people spiritually but to fulfil them with all their abilities. The way in which this occurs means that the Spirit works in the Old Testament, as Vos indicated differently.[24] The Spirit empowers in such a way as to enable the person himself/herself to use his/her abilities in the service of God. That Spirit is still the *ruach* of God and should not be directly associated with the Holy Spirit. It is the power of God to accomplish some tasks. This is associated with God's activity in the world and, in that respect, with the working of the Holy Spirit.

The New Testament highlights the personal nature of the Holy Spirit, who is also the Spirit that glorifies Christ and goes out from Christ. From the outset, the wonder of the relationship between Christ and the Holy Spirit is expressed with the immaculate conception. The Holy Spirit is the

---

22. Keener, *John*, 1.546–47.
23. O'Brien, *Hebrews*, 313.
24. Vos, *Heilige Gees*, 83–85.

Spirit of Christ, the Spirit who exists as the Third Person in the Trinity and the Spirit who keeps its own autonomy.

THE HOLY SPIRIT AND THE CHURCH

The Holy Spirit's work in the church is essential. There is no church without the Holy Spirit's persuasion and glorification of Jesus Christ. The Holy Spirit empowers the church to be church in Jesus Christ. This church must also witness to Jesus through love, service, care, and mediation.

Paul confirms the Spirit's unique work (1 Cor 2:10–16). As far as 1 Corinthians is concerned, DeSilva writes that there is a very important theme of how differences in culture and factions can be solved and how one must be in community with others.[25] The community is called together in Christ by God's gift of grace in order to honor each other. They should not boast of power, but of the things they have received from Christ. The preachers are thus a gift from God to the community, a sign of God's care for the new community, not on the basis of human considerations and their own honor. Even their mental faculty meant that there was a difference in opinion. Paul calls on them to acknowledge each other's gifts.

The true believer who knows God and his secrets has received the Spirit of Christ and knows Christ. The Spirit of God judges spiritual matters and helps the believer discover truth in God. God's wisdom judges human wisdom. The Spirit shows true wisdom.

Heyns has a unique approach to the church in relation to the world.[26] He opines that the church is not spun into a cocoon but that it must move out into the world. The church has a calling and a task in the world. Heyns confirms and emphasizes the idea of critical solidarity. The church is in solidarity with the world. The church's involvement with the world means that the church is in the world and a partner of the world.[27] The church and the world are not separate entities; they are mutually dependent. The church will remain involved and live in the world.

The soteriological working of the Holy Spirit means that the Holy Spirit works in the church. The church is the community called by God to be in a special close relationship with him. The Holy Spirit is continuously active in the church and emphasizes the wonder of God in a unique way.

25. DeSilva, *New Testament*, 568.
26. Heyns, *Dogmatiek*, 371.
27. Heyns, *Dogmatiek*, 371.

In terms of the special gifts or charismata, Heyns refers to the great diversity of gifts that are received from God's hand.[28] These gifts are meant for the believers, and, as far as the distribution of gifts is concerned, every believer does not receive the same. Not all gifts are given on the same level, but always to the glory of God and to the establishment of the community. Often, the duration of the gifts differs, and some gifts last longer than others. One can not infer from this that the Holy Spirit can not use his special gifts under special circumstances.

Heyns opines that there is no question of total rejection of gifts in that the work of the Holy Spirit stopped when the apostles ended their ministry. The Holy Spirit's work continues. Heyns discusses the different aspects of the Holy Spirit's work. First, the calling, the internal and external calling by the Holy Spirit whereby one is led out of darkness into God's wonderful light.[29] It is especially important to note that rebirth is the work of the Holy Spirit that starts new life in the heart of the elected.[30] Rebirth is, however, not a second activity besides faith. Rebirth creates faith, and through faith comes the renewal by the Holy Spirit. Faith is extremely important.[31] Heyns emphasizes that faith is a gift of the Spirit, that comes to us through God's gift.[32] Faith is an act of man, induced and emphasized by the Holy Spirit. It is also an answer by man to the Spirit of God in knowledge, faith, and obedience. This means that faith also becomes a total aspect of being human through which man reacts. Faith also means certainty and the glorification of God.[33] This is associated with justification, a unique judgment of God over humans, whereby God gives the wonderful reconciliation merits of Christ to him/her and he/she is then exonerated.[34] God's judgment is final, but justice means that the sinner is exonerated. It is a strange judgment when the initial nonbeliever is totally exonerated from sin. The justice, confirmation, and attribution of the exoneration are received in Christ through faith and not through work. Justice only takes place in faith, and

---

28. Heyns, *Dogmatiek*, 301.
29. Heyns, *Dogmatiek*, 304.
30. Heyns, *Dogmatiek*, 305.
31. Heyns, *Dogmatiek*, 307.
32. Heyns, *Dogmatiek*, 308.
33. Heyns, *Dogmatiek*, 310.
34. Heyns, *Dogmatiek*, 311.

this is established for God's eternal wonder of justice.[35] This also means that man must obey the law that creates new life.

Perseverance is an extremely important matter in theological thought.[36] The question is: Is it possible to persevere, and is it the Spirit itself that brings perseverance, or can humans indeed fall out of God's hand? Heyns describes this as the work of God that is continued in the life of humans so that we can ultimately persevere, because it is based in the Trinitarian work of God.[37] The Father, the Son, and the Holy Spirit effect the perseverance for humans and intervene for us because Christ, as High Priest, intervenes for us and the Holy Spirit helps us and all humans' weaknesses. The believer is called to the struggle and not to sit back and think that perseverance is simply given to him/her without him/her being involved in the perseverance.[38]

Vos also refers to the *ordo salutis* in the field of dogmatics and prefers the phrase "order of salvation," whereby the salvation of God is eschatologically conveyed by the Holy Spirit to the believer, enabling him/her to experience the fullness thereof.[39] The order of salvation needs to be explained. Rebirth is the important matter of salvation which, as the birth from above, is simply an act of re-creation.[40] Vos shows that the term "re-creation" conveys a very important climatological element.[41] He emphasizes the fact that rebirth is from above, a gift from God in the re-creation by the Holy Spirit. This affects the believer's whole life.

Vos points out that humans already exist, due to creation, but that the Holy Spirit also causes re-creation in the believer's life. The Holy Spirit's work of re-creation is thus important in rebirth. This implies that rebirth is a wonderful secret and broad concept.[42] The Holy Spirit conveys the events of salvation and the cross, but this does not imply that man must be dealt with passively, because rebirth is not only the beginning but also the experience of salvation. As one lives between two states, too early for heaven

---

35. Heyns, *Dogmatiek*, 313.
36. Heyns, *Dogmatiek*, 324.
37. Heyns, *Dogmatiek*, 325.
38. Heyns, *Dogmatiek*, 327.
39. Vos, *Heilige Gees*, 269.
40. Vos, *Heilige Gees*, 272.
41. Vos, *Heilige Gees*, 275.
42. Vos, *Heilige Gees*, 282.

and too late for earth, it is significant that the Holy Spirit is a sign of a temporary present, that the flesh will ultimately be renewed.

It must be pointed out that the Holy Spirit makes the church a church through rebirth. Rebirth is the way in which Jesus is brought into and blessed in the heart of the believer, when the Holy Spirit links Jesus' work to the heart of the believer. The church thus becomes a true church. This consciously acknowledges Jesus as the LORD. This is not a general matter that happens to all the people in the entire creation.

By redemption, I understand the total association with Jesus Christ through the Holy Spirit to the glorification of the Father, in whom total salvation of God is experienced, including life with Christ here and now and in eternal life with him. The glory that will be given in eternity can not be imagined. It includes the whole of life and the anticipation of being raised from the dead, for which we hope. Made holy through the Holy Spirit, we hope for God's justice.

Heyns writes that the church will also be utterly critical of the world from the relationship of faith with God and from the fact that it is chosen by God.[43] The church will also be critical of many things in the world. Being different in the world comes from God's calling to the church. He points out that the kingdom of God and the royal task of the church should be emphasized. Ultimately, it will also have a unique significance in mission.

The church's function of community is important. The Holy Spirit forms the unity of the church.[44] The unity lies on different levels, namely origin, calling, confession, witness, community, service, and organization. Heyns emphasizes that one should not dismiss these levels of the church.[45] There is room for unique expressions under specific circumstances.

In terms of the holiness of the church, Heyns emphasizes holiness as a status, action as obedience, and conflict.[46] He emphasizes the universality of God in time, of the world, of truth, of obedience.[47] He emphasizes apostolicity as commitment to both the word and Christ.

An important aspect is often mentioned concerning faith. Some regard that we are saved on the basis of the faith of Jesus Christ and not on the basis of our faith. Faith is a gift from God's hands. One must acknowledge

---

43. Heyns, *Dogmatiek*, 373.
44. Heyns, *Dogmatiek*, 377.
45. Heyns, *Dogmatiek*, 379.
46. Heyns, *Dogmatiek*, 380.
47. Heyns, *Dogmatiek*, 381.

that this faith is given to us only through the grace of God. This does not mean that we are saved on the basis of the faith of Jesus Christ. This is a wrong view in my opinion. We are saved on the basis of our faith in Jesus Christ; that is salvation. The faith that is given to us by Jesus Christ through the Holy Spirit is a faith in him and what he has done. Faith in Jesus Christ means that he gave his life for us, thus stressing his work and wonder for us. This wonder means that we obtain glory and final victory in Christ. This faith in Christ does not come from ourselves; it is the wonderful work of the Holy Spirit who facilitates this for us. The Holy Spirit thus brings us the new salvation. There is the danger of emphasizing objective salvation to such an extent that one totally misjudges the subjective acceptance thereof. This makes the work of the Holy Spirit *ex operato*, implying that the Holy Spirit works in such a way as to not emphasize that this also binds man to God in a unique way. In light of Dordt, this means that this must be understood in terms of predestination; only the wonder of God's grace makes this possible for us ultimately. The work of the Holy Spirit will have to be emphasized, but faith lies in the answer to God's salvation that is raised by the Holy Spirit, but that lies with man himself. Man believes in Jesus Christ and would thus receive salvation and redemption in Christ.

Galatians explains the way in which the believer is empowered. Tolmie points out that the Spirit determines the believer's life, as set out in Galatians.[48] Tolmie writes:

> If we formulate all of this in terms of the notion of discernment, the following seems to be the heart of the matter: Discernment is an activity practised by those who have been liberated by (and in) Christ, who have become slaves of love, and who live according to the Spirit. Such people will not merely follow their own inclinations (Gal. 5:17); rather their lives will express the fruit of the Spirit. To put it in another way: discernment practically implies bending one's will to that of the Spirit.[49]

Further,

> The fruit of the Spirit flows from the empowerment by the Spirit. (Gal 5:16–26)

DeSilva shows that Paul's core message to the Galatians is that the gospel means that Jesus Christ, the crucified, died for us in order to give us

---

48. Tolmie, "Galatians," 165.
49. Tolmie, "Galatians," 165.

the freedom to live before God.[50] Jesus died for our sin and through faith man can go to Jesus. The Holy Spirit gives the sign of salvation. One can live in freedom before God, but this does not mean profligacy, but rather service to each other.[51] From this follows the fruit of the Spirit.

The Spirit of God leads man to bear the fruit. It is also evident that the believer is no longer under the law, but that he or she is led by the Spirit. The accumulation of sinful practices and the fruit of the Spirit imply that each element is more strongly emphasized. Sin is so serious; the fruit of the Spirit is so good, as explained profusely. Those who practice sin and those who bear the fruit of the Spirit and belong to Jesus Christ differ from each other. The works of the Spirit of God stand against the sinful nature (the flesh). The fruit of the Spirit is directly in contrast with the works of the sinful nature (the flesh). Those who allow themselves to be led by the Spirit of God live in the glorification of God and know God. In order to belong to Christ, one needs to discard the sinful nature (the flesh) and show the fruit of the Spirit.

As far as the means of grace are concerned, Heyns refers to the immediate and indirect works of the Holy Spirit.[52] The one is the direct way: immediately in the heart of man without the use of any instruments the Holy Spirit works immediately. The Holy Spirit also works using the word and sacraments and how these are then supplemented by the Spirit.

The word is the first means whereby the Spirit speaks. The Holy Spirit uses the word to bring the kingdom of God to the people. The sacraments are the second important issue. The Holy Spirit works through the sacraments as the means that link us to Christ. Participation in the sacraments is important because one shares and participates in Christ's wonderful work.[53]

Holy Communion and baptism are two sacraments. Baptism brings a special message to humans through the working of the Holy Spirit.[54] The wonder of baptism, as sign and seal, ensures redemption in Jesus Christ. The baptism of a child refers to the covenant and acceptance of the covenant. The relationship between baptism and faith emphasizes this in a unique way.[55] Holy Communion refers to the work of Christ. The words have a

50. DeSilva, *New Testament*, 496–517.
51. DeSilva, *New Testament*, 517.
52. Heyns, *Dogmatiek*, 329.
53. Heyns, *Dogmatiek*, 337.
54. Heyns, *Dogmatiek*, 339.
55. Heyns, *Dogmatiek*, 341.

unique meaning because the deeds of salvation are given to the person at Holy Communion.[56] Holy Communion is about the wonder of the confirmation of the word of God. Heyns also emphasizes the importance of the Holy Spirit's relationship with the church. The Holy Spirit forms the church as a community of holy people and calls for faith in Christ. The Holy Spirit shows that the church is the chosen nation of God, the body of Christ, the bride of Christ.[57] The church is in a threefold relationship: to God,[58] to the Son, and especially to God the Holy Spirit.[59] The Holy Spirit binds humans to Jesus Christ; emphasizes the significance of community in Christ; binds us to the kingdom of God;[60] emphasizes that Christ is the King of the church; links with the word; and makes the word visible. Humans are also sent out into the world to be part of the world's life. The Holy Spirit emphasizes that we must go out into the world to proclaim the Word of God. The Holy Spirit also binds one person to others and binds them to the future expectations given by God. Not only was Christ the first to rise from the dead. The Holy Spirit is called "the first" because he binds us to the eschatological community.[61]

The Holy Spirit lets us conquer sin and makes us children of God (1 John 3:9, 24). Yarbrough explains: "Believers know, by the Spirit that God (or Christ) gives them, that they abide in Christ and Christ in them as they keep the commandments to trust and love."[62]

The Holy Spirit empowers in a wonderful way and conveys the true word of God to the servant of Christ. The Holy Spirit makes prayer possible as the most important part of gratitude. Prayer is the culmination of faith. The believer is called into the church to believe and to pray.

With reference to Romans 8:26, Moo writes:

> I take it that Paul is saying, then, that our failure to know God's will and consequent inability to petition God specifically and assuredly is met by God's Spirit, who himself expresses to God those intercessory petitions that perfectly match the will of God. When we do not know what to pray for—yes, even when we pray for

---

56. Heyns, *Dogmatiek*, 346.
57. Heyns, *Dogmatiek*, 359.
58. Heyns, *Dogmatiek*, 363.
59. Heyns, *Dogmatiek*, 365.
60. Heyns, *Dogmatiek*, 365.
61. Heyns, *Dogmatiek*, 366.
62. Yarbrough, *1–3 John*, 215–17.

things that are not best for us—we need not despair, for we can depend on the Spirit's ministry of perfect intercession "on our behalf." Here is one potent source for that "patient fortitude" with which we are to await our glory (v. 25); that our failure to understand God's purposes and plans, to see "the beginning from the end," does not mean that effective, powerful prayer for our specific needs is absent.[63]

THE NEW DISPENSATION OF EXONERATION BY THE SON IS THE TIME OF THE SPIRIT

> No, a person is a Jew who is one inwardly; and circumcision is circumcision of the heart, by the Spirit, not by the written code. Such a person's praise is not from other people, but from God. (Rom 2:29)[64]

DeSilva refers to Romans and points to three recent movements.[65] First, as in Paul's other letters, there is an objective and direction in the letter to the Romans. Secondly, the letter highlights community. Earlier, the emphasis was on individual salvation. Now, Romans also mentions joint salvation. Thirdly, Romans should not be preferred to the other letters that should be examined in terms of the theology of Paul.

DeSilva explains that Paul conveys a very specific message in Romans.[66] First, the Jews and the pagans should be one community in Jesus Christ who wants to save all. The one can not be preferred to the other. The unity of mankind in Adam and Abraham, Adam and Christ, is very strongly emphasized, including radical grace. Obedience in faith and God's loyalty to Israel are also emphasized. God wants to bring his wonderful salvation to the community in order to achieve a shared life in the Christian community in obedience to God. DeSilva writes:

> In each of Paul's letters apocalyptic orientation shines through. This is no less true for Romans. For example, in Romans 8:18–25, the cosmic scope of God's redemption, extending to creation itself and not merely the individuals inhabiting creation, shines through. The apocalyptic vision reminds us ever that God's purposes for

---

63. Moo, *Romans*, 522–26.
64. See also Rom 5:5; 7:6; 8:2–16.
65. DeSilva, *New Testament*, 599.
66. DeSilva, *New Testament*, 606.

God's creation are broad and all-encompassing, and that they are still being worked out in the present and into the future. The believer's posture also involved longing and waiting. While we have been incorporated into Christ and have peace with God and the endowment of the Spirit, we still groan with creation as our bodies are subject to mortality—to disease, decay and death—as we wait for the redemption at the resurrection (Romans 8:17–25).[67]

The implications of the repeated use of sin and sinful nature is that these can be overcome only by the Holy Spirit in Jesus. True freedom is found in the Spirit. The law of sinful nature leads to death, but freedom is found in Christ through the Holy Spirit. Hostility towards God is overcome by the Spirit who highlights the wonder of redemption. The Spirit lives in the believer and it is, therefore, possible to conquer sin. This leads to true filiation of God.

Romans 8:22–27 is important, as it includes three forms of groans, namely creation (verse 22), the believers (verse 23), and the Holy Spirit (verse 26). The groans of creation for the desire that those who have received the Spirit will be revealed.

Romans 8:23 is also important in this instance. Creation and those of us who have received the Spirit as the first gift from God also groan. We long for the moment when God will announce that he has adopted us as his children. He will redeem us.

The Holy Spirit is the first grace. As the harvest is devoted to God with the first grace that is given to him, the Holy Spirit is given humans to make eschatological glory possible.[68] The Spirit as the first grace makes the future possible for humans. The Spirit is also *arrabon*, or pledge. Vos points to three meanings, namely security in agreements, first payment or deposit, and caution money.[69] Vos chooses the concept of "loan," which strongly emphasizes the eschatological aspect.[70] The Holy Spirit thus ensures that eternity will be given. The Holy Spirit already seals the believer's eternal destination.[71] Abundant promises are conveyed in that the Holy Spirit is the loan.[72]

67. DeSilva, *New Testament*, 638.
68. Vos, *Heilige Gees*, 254.
69. Vos, *Heilige Gees*, 256.
70. Vos, *Heilige Gees*,:258.
71. Vos, *Heilige Gees*, 258.
72. Vos, *Heilige Gees*, 259.

Creation also groans. The repeated groans imply the craving that the Holy Spirit will reveal the children of God and that total redemption will occur. The Spirit intervenes and reveals the children of God. The Spirit intervenes for the believers, thus witnessing who the children of God are. The wonder of the Spirit is up against sinful nature. The Spirit and the spirit of the believer prove that they are children of God. The Spirit is also the gift of God and intervenes for the believer with inexpressible pleads. All this includes hope. The incredible expectation is that God will give true life, but also hope, for the believer.

God as the Father in His Love and Glory

GOD THE FATHER

It is essential to consider the Father and mission. It is crucial that the church witnesses God as Father. This wonderful witness acknowledges God the Father's glory and wonder. The Fatherhood of God is not a gender issue but a confession of his love.

Van de Beek points out that patrology is essential, because one must think anew of the Father.[1] One can talk about God the Father because the Old Testament's numerous metaphors confirm his Fatherhood. There are many references to God as Father in the New Testament, the Synoptic Gospels, Acts, Paul, John, and the letters. The idea that God can be addressed as Abba Father is especially significant. God as Father is nearby. An important indication of the Father is that God is greatly exalted.[2] As Father, he is also merciful. Jeremiah already indicated that he provides for the needs of his children.[3]

Van de Beek explains that there is a difference of opinion on power and authority. The patriarchal community in which God is called Father, points to submission. Abba is then viewed in light of the highest authority and total submission. Forgiving mercy occurs, but this is approached from the judgment. Van de Beek indicates that the Father is the LORD of heaven and earth.[4] He is holy and fair.

---

1. Van de Beek, *Mijn Vader, uw Vader*, 1–20.
2. Van de Beek, *Mijn Vader, uw Vader*, 52.
3. Van de Beek, *Mijn Vader, uw Vader*, 53.
4. Van de Beek, *Mijn Vader, uw Vader*, 54.

In Romans 8:15, "Abba" implies freedom. Those who now live in Christ are free to be and to live as the children of God. They are safe in the love of God.[5] The title "Abba" is first and foremost the title of the Son and the Spirit to the Father. The eschatological community of God joins in the Trinitarian prayer. By praying, the community simply approaches the Father through the Spirit, through and in Jesus Christ.

Durand does not mention a separate patrology.[6] He points to the different opinions on God throughout the centuries. God's transcendence and immanence are important. One should not proffer an abstract idea of God. One must talk about God as he reveals himself and how he introduces himself in his revelation. God is always more than his revelation.[7]

There are various ways in which one can understand God as person. God is not an ordinary person like a human person, yet God introduces himself in his anthropomorphism as person. In talking about God as person, one must note specifically that God addresses man from his glory as God the Father. God is in a specific new relationship with humans.[8]

God's love must be seen in Christ. God's wrath can not be placed on the same level as love.[9] One must address the issue of the suffering God (theopaschism) by showing that God is involved in the suffering of man. God is troubled in Christ.[10] There is also mention of God's sorrow.[11]

Migliore points out that the Trinity also confirms that God is personified in relationships. He emphasizes that God is acknowledged in a special way as the triune God, namely the Father as Father of the LORD Jesus Christ through the Holy Spirit. God lives in this community in a much stronger relationship than any other relationship one can ever imagine in our own human life. He confirms the confession that God is triune in his essential self-giving love that strengthens and embraces us in our weakness.[12]

When referring to the attributes or characteristics of God, Migliore shows how difficult it is to highlight one specific aspect.[13] God's love can

---

5. Van de Beek, *Mijn Vader, uw Vader*, 57.
6. Durand, *Lewende God*, 9–10.
7. Durand, *Lewende God*, 47.
8. Durand, *Lewende God*, 60.
9. Durand, *Lewende God*, 90.
10. Durand, *Lewende God*, 99.
11. Durand, *Lewende God*, 100.
12. Migliore, *Faith Seeking Understanding*, 76.
13. Migliore, *Faith Seeking Understanding*, 85.

both hurt and not be conquerable. God chooses in his grace, and this can only be understood as the incredible love of God for the world in Jesus Christ through the Holy Spirit. The aim of choosing is to call people for God and not necessarily the individual person's salvation or the preference of some nations. The choosing grace of God is accompanied by his fair judgment. These are not parallel lines, as is often highlighted in double predestination.[14]

It is essential to mention God the Father and mission, as questions in respect of God's judgment and love are at issue. God is love, according to Scripture. What is this love? How can it be conveyed to the world in need? Is the Father a God of love? In this regard, what is the relationship between the Father and the Son? What should our relationship to God the Father be like when he is served and worshipped? How can mission proclaim and realize the praise, honor, and sovereignty of the Father?

To speak more specifically about God as Father, one must examine more references to him in detail.

THE LORD'S PRAYER

There is no better place to start considering the Father than with the Lord's Prayer, which points to the profound relationship with the Father. The prayer confirms the glory of the Father. This is crucial for mission. One can definitely talk about mission only when the Father is known. Mission glorifies the triune God with praise, honor, and glory to the Father. There is no mission without honor to the Father. Acknowledging the Father determines mission.

The Lord's Prayer clearly indicates the relationship with the Father. This prayer provides a glimpse of God the Father. One enters into a wonderful relationship with God. He is the Father. This is linked with prayers that glorify him, as one can turn to him. Turner writes:

> Matthew 6:9-10 convincingly shows that one should not pray primarily in order to receive goods and services from God but to render service to God. Prayer is not first and foremost an exercise to vindicate the disciple's causes, meet the disciple's needs, fulfil the disciple's desires, or solve the disciple's problems. Rather, one's priority must be the promotion of God's reputation, the advancement of God's rule, and the performance of God's will. These three

---

14. Migliore, *Faith Seeking Understanding*, 88–91.

petitions are essentially one expression of burning desire to see the Father honored on earth as he is already honored in heaven (cf. Rev. 4–5). The disciples' hope is not escapism—they do not look to leave the earth for an ethereal heavenly existence. Rather, they look for a concrete existence in which heaven comes to earth, and they seek heaven's interests on earth today as they anticipate a time when God's reign on earth will be consummated (Matt. 13:40–43; 16:27–28; 19:28–30; 25:34).[15]

Luz confirms this:

> Many people can find themselves in its formulations, because it does not prescribe to praying people what wishes, hopes, or views they must have. To that degree, not only does it presuppose grace by addressing God as it does; it is itself an expression of God's grace and nearness. By including many people in its words, it makes prayer possible. One might say, with some exaggeration, that it is not a sign by which the circle of disciples is to be recognized but an expression of the grace that precedes the circle of disciples.[16]

The Heidelberg Catechism Questions 118–29 clearly express the honor of the Father.[17]

In terms of the Lord's Prayer, Van de Beek points out that the community prays together and orientates themselves into prayer.[18] One prays as a living member of the community, but this is also the most important part of gratitude. It offers thanks to God.[19] Regarding the holiness of God's name, Van de Beek shows that it is about the glory of God, about God himself, and about taking the glorification of God seriously.[20]

According to Van de Beek, "Thy kingdom come" is about the liberating power and the right to pray of the God of Israel.[21] This may never be separated from the kingship of God[22] and is only visible in a serving community.[23]

---

15. Turner, *Matthew*, 195.
16. Luz, *Matthew 1–7*, 326.
17 "Heidelberg Catechism."
18. Van de Beek, *Mijn Vader, uw Vader*, 341.
19. Van de Beek, *Mijn Vader, uw Vader*, 342.
20. Van de Beek, *Mijn Vader, uw Vader*, 349, 361.
21. Van de Beek, *Mijn Vader, uw Vader*, 365.
22. Van de Beek, *Mijn Vader, uw Vader*, 366.
23. Van de Beek, *Mijn Vader, uw Vader*, 369.

"Thy will be done" is about the fact that Jesus prayed that the will of God will be done. The congregation prays together because it is imbued with God's Spirit.[24]

Van de Beek opines that the daily bread means sharing in the sanctification of the name of God, of Jesus and the kingship in history of God's will.[25] It concerns first and foremost Jesus himself, who becomes the bread of life.

Van de Beek points out that forgiveness of sins is not about cheap grace, but about the expensive grace of God.[26] Because we are forgiven in Christ, we can also forgive others.[27] "Lead us not into temptation" means that we must simply obey him.[28]

Van de Beek concludes by asking, "What does it mean to pray?" As children of God, we can talk with God.[29] The nearness and intimate relationship with God bear our prayers.

God is the Father who exists in his glory and who lives in heaven, from which he reigns. One must also ask that his name be sanctified. God's name is not sanctified everywhere on earth. There are many places and occasions where the name of God is misused. The Bible mentions stories where God's name is neither acknowledged nor sanctified. In the Old Testament, God's special name is YHWH, and it is emphasized in a very unique way. God's name was so holy in the Old Testament for the Israelites that they often did not utter the name but merely referred to the name to indicate God. When one asks in the Lord's Prayer that God's name be sanctified, this conveys a very specific attribute of God. God is holy, and his name must be sanctified. In the world of the Old Testament, a person's name meant more than simply the person's specific meaning, and God's name is, in this sense, also holy. This means that one must acknowledge God as God. The Father is acknowledged as the one who is Holy: "Holy, holy, holy is the LORD" (Rev 4:8). God is the absolute, the holy who reigns, who rules in his glory. Because he is the Father and is, in the first instance, addressed as Father, this also has significance for those who kneel before God and worship him, thus acknowledging that he the Father is holy.

---

24. Van de Beek, *Mijn Vader, uw Vader*, 375.
25. Van de Beek, *Mijn Vader, uw Vader*, 382, 384.
26. Van de Beek, *Mijn Vader, uw Vader*, 387.
27. Van de Beek, *Mijn Vader, uw Vader*, 390.
28. Van de Beek, *Mijn Vader, uw Vader*, 393.
29. Van de Beek, *Mijn Vader, uw Vader*, 413.

The second prayer, "thy kingdom come," is linked to what Jesus proclaimed. The kingdom of God has come, emphasizing that the Father also brings the kingdom of God near us. We thus ask that the kingdom of God come. The kingdom comes from and is determined by the Father who sent his Son. That kingdom is not a worldly kingdom; it is different from the kingdoms of the world. How did the Father send his Son? In the form of a man who was ultimately crucified. This kingdom of God that must come comes through the cross. The Father is the one who, in this sense, allows the kingdom to come. The Father and the Son have a special relationship in this instance, in that the Son can also ask that the kingdom of God come.

The third prayer specifically shows us how we must think about the Father: "Thy will be done on earth as it is in heaven." This shows that from the heavenly glory of God the Father there must be glory for the people on earth, so that God's will can be fully done. Heyns pointed out the differences between the advice of God, where God in his glory as Father disposes of and rules everything, and the will of God, which does not occur on earth everywhere because sin is not the will of God and God is not the author of sin.[30] God in his advice still uses sin so that sin can be used to punish and reveal the sin. In the prayer that the will of God be done as in heaven, the will of God is absolute and wonderful. In the heavenly glory of God the Father who lives in heavenly glory, there is no mention that the will shall not be done. The will of God must be done here on earth through the wonder of his Son who died on the cross and who was risen from the dead. The will of God is thus most profoundly bound to what Jesus does on the cross. On the cross, Jesus shows the full significance of the will of God that is totally done. On the cross, the fullness of the will of God can also be accounted for. With God's will on the cross for salvation and redemption, Jesus himself, in obedience, lets the will of God be done. Jesus obediently accomplishes God's advice and presents himself as the holy offering (according to Hebrews) so that God's will can be done. Hagner writes:

> The LORD's Prayer thus centers on the large issues of God's redemptive program rather than on more mundane matters. The disciples are to pray above all for the realization of God's eschatological program on earth. Most of the petitions in the prayer are dominated by this concern for the end time. Yet, at the same time, the petitions have implications for the present . . . The one who prays the LORD's Prayer prays thus from a perspective of one

---

30. Heyns, *Dogmatiek*, 205.

who is involved in the great redemptive drama that is beginning to unfold in the Gospel narrative itself. The measure of eschatological fulfilment already realized focuses one's thoughts and desires upon the consummation of God's purposes as well as upon the consciousness and importance of present discipleship.[31]

"Give us this day our daily bread" makes us dependent on the Father. In his dependence on God the Father, man is called upon to live before God; to put out his hands to God, in order to receive help and guidance from God; to pray for his most basic need of daily bread from God, so that God in his care and love for man can care for man. The Father's special care, his caring for man and for the believer who calls him our Father, is clear. It is true that this is also associated with the holy communion,[32] but it must also be interpreted more widely to include the full existence of man.

"And forgive us our trespasses." The Father makes it possible to be forgiven from sin. This forgiveness can only take place based on the fact that the Lord's Prayer must also be viewed in the context of the cross of Jesus. Although the Lord's Prayer also mentions "as we forgive those who trespass against us," this is not a condition for the forgiveness of God. God does not forgive because we forgive, but he forgives us so that we can also forgive. This prayer shows what really takes place when we can experience this new relationship that comes from Christ and the forgiveness of Christ. Thus, forgiveness becomes a radical reality that comes from the Father, and this reality is only visible on the cross in Jesus Christ.

This also means that the Father calls us to live on account of his salvation, care, and charitableness and that we should not live on account of the world or of evil.

"Let us not enter into temptation" indicates that we should not reason from the temptation, but from the redemption in Jesus Christ. The wonderful redemption is the result of abandoning temptation and redeeming man from evil. This is only possible from the near and unique relationship with the Living God. Only when we are in this unique relationship with the Living God can there be redemption from evil (Eph 6). This specific prayer shows that, in his love and care, the Father cares for those who live on earth. The Father wants to assure those who believe in him that he will not lead them into temptation because he himself does not lead anybody into temptation, but he redeems from evil.

31. Hagner, *Matthew*, 1–13.
32. Van de Beek, *Mijn Vader, uw Vader*, 193.

"For thine is the kingdom, the power and the glory, for ever and ever" does not occur in the vast majority of texts, as it is considered to be a later addition. Despite this, it can be pointed out how this conveys the full significance of how his kingdom, his power, and his glory are visible for eternity in what he does. The Lord's Prayer is especially significant for understanding patrology, for which we say God as Father is the wonderful Father who brings salvation.

When we worship the Father, we always give thanks and praise to the Father because we must acknowledge his glory and his goodness.

THE LOVE OF THE FATHER

The parable of the prodigal son, Luke 15:11–32, expresses the love of the Father most profoundly.

There are a few important matters regarding the parable of the prodigal son. DeSilva points to some main aspects in Luke that are important for addressing the parable.[33] The sign of the new community is the restoration of the sinner. The community's love is shown by reaching out to the sinner who repents, and this is possible through restoring the relationship with God. There are a number of references to how God in a specific way restores the relationship between people and how God's righteousness heals them of their sin. Regarding the prodigal son, DeSilva writes:

> Those opposed to Jesus' calling of the sinner (indeed, to God's attempts to restore the sinner) are put to shame at the end of the chapter. They are seen to be reflected in the elder son who refused to share in the father's joy, standing off at a distance and grumbling against the father's mercy (Lk 15:25–32).[34]

DeSilva also describes the way in which one has to react to this:

> In sum, the church is to reflect the character and heart of Jesus, not by separating itself from sinners but by reaching out to them, calling them to repentance and newness of life, being the agent of God's continued restoration of the lost and wayward, and that becoming the source of ongoing joy in heaven.[35]

---

33. DeSilva, *New Testament*, 323.
34. DeSilva, *New Testament*, 324.
35. DeSilva, *New Testament*, 324.

It is obvious that the son himself is guilty for moving away from God and rejecting God. God must then judge his life. When he asks his father to give him everything that belongs to him and then goes to a distant land, he turns his back not only on his father but also on God. On his return, his father is the symbol of God in Jesus Christ who, as Father, welcomes the child back. He radiates the unbelievable forgiveness of his love and his special care for the one who comes to him. He accepts the child with great love and blessing with his forgiveness and goodness. This shows the full and abundant love of the Father. The fattened calf is slaughtered; there are celebrations; there is music. The father also mentions the reason for this: the child had been dead, but they found him again. God the Father is like this in Jesus Christ.

The other son, however, does not acknowledge that the father is a father of love. He wants to act in a hard and radical manner. He demands that he be judged and that the prodigal son be affected by the judgment of both the father and God. The father, as an image of God the Father, shows extreme love. Liefeld explains:

> As in v. 2 . . . by telling the story Jesus identifies himself with God in his loving attitude to the lost. He represents God in his mission, the accomplishment of which should elicit joy from those who share the Father's compassion. The parable is one of the world's supreme masterpieces of storytelling. Its details are vivid; they reflect actual customs and legal procedures and build up the story's emotional and spiritual impact. But the expositor must resist the tendency to allegorize the wealth of detail that gives the story its remarkable verisimilitude. The main point of the parable—that God gladly receives repentant sinners—must not be obscured.[36]

Nolland writes:

> This large parable completes the section 15:1–32. The "joy in heaven" of the earlier parables prepares us for thinking of the parable father in close connection with God and also causes us to come to the parable with images of discovery, repentance, and shared joy. The parable itself helps us to see that in the ministry of Jesus, sinners who in their need draw near are finding the free and generous love of the heavenly Father. Despite the elder son's misgivings, there is nothing here that should disturb those who are concerned with holy living; here the faithful are regaining lost

---

36. Liefeld, "Luke," 987.

brothers whom they should welcome and whose restoration they should celebrate.[37]

The prodigal son is embraced and included in the glory that comes from God. God also accepts man in his deepest misery. This acceptance is visible in Jesus Christ on the cross. Humans can experience the wonder of God's absolute salvation and redemption only through the cross, bringing hope for man.

One can not talk about the love of God if it can not be viewed in light of the cross. One would have to ask: "Where is the God of love?" One sees the love of God in the cross, even to those who committed suicide. The cross expresses hope for the depressed and anxious person. His love also offers that person salvation and redemption. The cross is the key. Always the cross. Always the key. For this reason, one must be cautious about any superficial understanding of the love of God.[38]

Rob Bell's book *Love Wins: At the Heart of Life's Big Questions* is in many respects Marcionistic and does not show an understanding of the fact that the judgment of God is also a reality, and that God ultimately accomplishes his judgment.[39] On the issue of the love of God, Bell asks the question as to whether one can really talk about a God of love if there is so much emphasis on the fact that there is a hell. Bell asks: "What is understood by heaven and the concept that people go to heaven?" He also asks whether it is truly right to think that a person such as, for example, Gandhi, is in hell. What must be understood by "heaven"? He concludes that heaven is not necessarily a moment of change in which we receive glory. Bell points out that a big question, according to him, is not where we will end, but how we now live in the world, in reality.[40]

Besides Bell's *Love Wins* there is Galli's book, *God Wins: Heaven, Hell, and Why the Good News Is Better than Love Wins*.[41] Galli's argument is that one can only talk about God's love when one also considers the depth of misery. Galli refers to the fact that God must be viewed as the Creator and agent of salvation,[42] but he shows that God must not simply be viewed as

---

37. Nolland, *Luke 9:21—18:34*, 789.
38. Van de Beek, *Mijn Vader, uw Vader*, 73.
39. Bell, *Love Wins*, 1–19.
40. Bell, *Love Wins*, 197.
41. Galli, *God Wins*, 1–14.
42. Galli, *God Wins*, 18.

agent of love[43] if one does not understand the fullness of life with God.[44] Galli emphasizes the fact that the love of God is indeed bigger because it includes the wonder of the offer of Jesus Christ on the cross who takes away the sins. He describes the total wonder of God's redemption.[45] Intense love is that God saves us in a wonderful way from sin and that we must understand the bad news of the sin in order to be able to truly understand redemption. Heaven is different from what Bell suggests, and not only an expectation of the here and now. Heaven is also an expectation that is a reality for us because we can experience the glory thereof in God.

Galli describes the wonder of the kingdom of heaven because that is where God is.[46] Because God emphasizes the glory that is being expected, there will be redemption, and the honor and worship of God will be the main issue.[47] The true experience of heaven is when one experiences the full love of God when one is redeemed in Christ from the reality of sin and misery. In terms of hell and judgment, Galli writes that one can not fail to appreciate this,[48] because the fact is that God is also a God of judgment, a lawyer whom we can trust.[49] The true story of the Bible also includes that the God of grace and love is the God of judgment, as clearly stated in the Bible.

In that respect, Galli's book approximates the biblical image of God and the biblical message. In the modern world, people do not want to know about the judgment of God, about the cross. Meanwhile, people are anxious and in need. It must be noted that one can know God only in his love in the way in which Jesus Christ on the cross brings redemption.

The main problem with Dawkins's *The God Delusion* is that he does not understand that the God of the Bible reveals him in his love in terms of his relationship with humans and in what he does on the cross.[50] It is not a solution for modern humans to exclude the entire confession regarding God and then to think that there is a solution for the need of the world. Humans can not provide an answer from reality itself or an answer if she/he excludes God and then thinks that she/he will lead an easy life. It is

43. Galli, *God Wins*, 24.
44. Galli, *God Wins*, 30.
45. Galli, *God Wins*, 59–76.
46. Galli, *God Wins*, 86.
47. Galli, *God Wins*, 87.
48. Galli, *God Wins*, 96.
49. Galli, *God Wins*, 98.
50. Dawkins, *The God Delusion*, 1–30.

thus very clear that those who exclude God's message do so because they do not understand the depth of the gospel correctly. In dealing with the image of God, Dawkins and others like him often tend to create an image of God for themselves from their own understanding. This is only possible if humans live in reasonable prosperity. It is not possible, if one lives in dire need in the world, to follow atheistic approaches and to consider that one can go through life without any problems. Dawkins's idea that one can live a full life without God is often only possible for those who live in reasonable prosperity. This means that one is, in fact, confronted with the problem of existence in the world, which can only be addressed from Jesus Christ's death on the cross.

For justice to be done to God's being, one must also write about the judgment of the Father. See Matthew 7:21; 10:33; and John 2:16; 5:45; 6:27; 8:39, 41–44. In John 8:42–45, we see that one can not talk about God the Father without also realizing that God is the Holy God who judges in his holiness. God is not only the Holy God; he also judges as God. As God, he is also bound to confirm the glory of his majesty. He proclaims to us that one must be pure in one's life before God. When one has sinned, God judges. There is a unique link between the will of God the Father and his glory. Jesus will also renounce those who renounce him, and he will do so before the Father who is in heaven. He will not acknowledge them in front of the Father. The Father will judge them. Those who do not acknowledge him and those who do not glorify Jesus will not acknowledge the Father and will not be included in the glory of the Father. The judgment comes from the Father; it is given to the Son so that the Son can judge. The Son also judges in the case of the cleansing of the temple, when his Father's honor is affected. This means that the judgment of the Father and the judgment of the Son are linked and that such judgment must be highlighted. The judgment is further fulfilled when some do not wish to acknowledge that Jesus comes from the Father and say that Abraham is their Father. Jesus thus corrects them and shows that he and the Father are One, and that he proclaims the glorification of his Father.

Jesus then indicates that, in the judgment of God, it is important to acknowledge the Father and, in doing so, they would also acknowledge him. There is a very special relationship that can only be understood if they also acknowledge it. Jesus mentions that those who reject him are children of the devil because God is their Father. Because they do not wish to

GOD AS THE FATHER IN HIS LOVE AND GLORY

acknowledge that he is the LORD who comes from the Father, that specific relationship between Father and Son is thus undervalued.

The section on the good shepherd (John 10) provides very strong indications of Jesus' relationship with the Father. The thief steals, slaughters, and destroys. Those who steal and slaughter are nudged, if they do not acknowledge and confirm the glorification of God the Father and the majesty of Jesus. When they allege that he does not come from the Father, he says that they use blasphemous words, because he calls God his Father. They must know that he does the works of his Father and, if they do not believe in him because of that, they also reject the Father. It is expressly pointed out that whoever hates him also hates the Father. There is a unique relationship, but it is clear that the Father will judge those who do not believe and do not acknowledge the wonder of redemption.

The Father does not always judge to destroy, but often to uplift. The discipline of the Father leads to upliftment and renewal. Not only the earthly fathers but also the Father in heaven discipline so that people can get closer to God.

Hebrews 12:7–9 (especially v. 7) expresses this well: "Endure hardship as discipline; God is treating you as his children. For, what children are not disciplined by their father?"

Van de Beek always wants to view the love of God in relation to Christ. One can talk about this only in relation to Christ. One can understand that God is love only if one sees this in Christ. God himself is offered in Christ in this struggle in the world. As such, he reveals himself.[51]

God would never have been able to reveal his love if the world was not like it is because he must reveal his love in the cross. He must bring the history of the world to us through the cross. He does not love in an abstract manner, but he is visible in his Son.[52] Van de Beek writes that one can only consider these profound issues. In God's grace, one sees the light of love, but this is about God's faith, faith in everything.[53]

Van de Beek explains that one could never understand God's love if God did not reveal his redemptive love in Christ.[54] His saving love is only visible in Christ. He points out that the rulers of the world reveal the

---

51. Van de Beek, *Mijn Vader, uw Vader*, 424.
52. Van de Beek, *Mijn Vader, uw Vader*, 425.
53. Van de Beek, *Mijn Vader, uw Vader*, 429.
54. Van de Beek, *Mijn Vader, uw Vader*, 437.

tension in this world, but it ends in the death of both Jesus and man.⁵⁵ The resurrection of Christ totally renews the world.

What is extremely important in Van de Beek's approach is that one can not imagine a God who does not deal directly with the world.⁵⁶ The God who is often proffered in modern times is the loving God who can not really get involved in the deepest need of man in his/her suffering. The loving God is the God of songs of praise, and people are swept away by spiritual rapture that ultimately proffers prosperity theology. Why is God the God of love? Because God connects with people in Jesus Christ on the cross. Van de Beek thus writes that God is visible on the cross in this world.⁵⁷ For this reason, Paul knows of nothing else but that Jesus is the crucified. Van de Beek starts with the cross and, to him, the significance of the cross is radial and absolute. Only in this way can one truly talk about and know God. In the real world, a superficial approach is not really possible.

One can not talk of the love of God in this terrible world without looking intensively at the cross that conveys this love. Only the cross of Jesus Christ can advise as to the depth of the misery of the world, and only in it can one find redemption and hope for a new life and a new relationship. Only when one looks at the cross can one see the God of love. There is no other way of talking about God's love than the love of God on the cross.

Van de Beek emphasizes that the resurrection of Jesus Christ provides an answer.⁵⁸ God crucially proves the fact that he is God in that Jesus was resurrected. In his resurrection, he provides us with new hope.

Van de Beek clearly explains that the solace of the cross is the true solace.⁵⁹ On the cross, God reveals himself and takes on humanity's suffering. Ultimately, this also leads to the resurrection that creates new hope. This means that we are safe in Jesus Christ to belong to the church and to experience the unity of the church and the message.⁶⁰ One is not fear-stricken because one is held in God's wonder through Jesus Christ.

The essential question is the love of God. For Van de Beek, this is about the cross of Jesus Christ. Only from the cross can one understand God's true love and how one can reach out to others. Indeed, this argument

55. Van de Beek, *Mijn Vader, uw Vader*, 443.
56. Van de Beek, *Altijd dat Kruis*, 11–12.
57. Van de Beek, *Altijd dat Kruis*, 11–12.
58. Van de Beek, *Altijd dat Kruis*, 85.
59. Van de Beek, *Altijd dat Kruis*, 91
60. Van de Beek, *Altijd dat Kruis*, 102–03.

seems to be true. One sees the love of God only in the cross. One could not see it any differently in this world of unbelievable grief; poverty, suffering, and grief from COVID-19 with consequences for the whole of humanity. One can but confess one's sins and ask that God, in the cross of Jesus Christ, will come through the Holy Spirit to enable one to experience the wonder of resurrection and the new life in Christ. This can only happen when one experiences the fullness of the cross.

THE COVENANT. GOD AS FATHER OF SALVATION

The implication of the covenant in Genesis 12, 15, and 22 is that God as Father will act for Abraham and will bless him with his special nearness so that he can also be a blessing for others. The Fatherhood of God is also emphasized in other respects towards David and Solomon.[61] In Psalm 89:27, God is addressed as Father. Isaiah 63:16 also emphasizes that God is the Father. This is strongly expressed in 2 Corinthians 6:18: "and I will be a Father to you, and you shall be sons and daughters to me, says the LORD Almighty."

The covenant is very important. God is the Father of salvation, as confirmed in the covenant. God says: "I will be a God for you and you will be a child for me." God will be the Father to the child and be with him/her. This creates a whole new relationship with the child. He takes him/her to the wonder of his salvation and redemption. He is the Father who is concerned, who cares, who shows his love, and who is also the Father of the covenant. On the one hand, there is the institution of the covenant. He is the LORD God who also made Abraham from Ur of the Chaldeans come to the Holy Land. He is the LORD God who led the Israelites from the slave house in Egypt. Later, he led them from exile back to their land. For this reason, they must come and live in a specific relationship before him. It is essential that man also acts in the covenant as God's covenant partner. God is the absolute covenant partner, the one who enters into the covenant. As Father, he calls his child. Abraham is called to answer the covenant stipulations. Abraham can not enter into the covenant, but he acknowledges the covenant glory of God. Abraham appears before God and states that he also acknowledges God. Before he could do anything for the circumcision, God calls to him in the covenant: "I will be a God for you and you must be my child."

---

61. See 1 Chr 17:13; 22:10; 28:6.

The Father must be glorified and emulated because he is the wonderful God who reveals himself in his love and care. It is very clear that the light must shine from the life of the believer so that she/he can glorify the Father who is in heaven. The Father is near his children. For this reason, they are called children of God who must be as absolute as the Father in heaven, because they are simply in this unique relationship with the Father and must also acknowledge the Father's glory and that the Father is good. God rules as Father over man in his unique way. He is holy and makes holy because we are all from one Father. Jesus is not shy to be called brother of the believers.

Many texts point to God's care. See Matthew 6:26: "Look at the birds of the air; they do not sow or reap or store away in barns, and yet your heavenly Father feeds them. Are you not much more valuable than they?" And Matthew 10:29: "Are not two sparrows sold for a penny? Yet not one of them will fall to the ground outside your Father's care."

God is also the Father who cares and is concerned. Already in Matthew it is stated very clearly that he is the Living God who is concerned for those who believe in him. He cares for them more than for the wild birds that neither sow nor reap, more than the grass of the field, because he is the Father who is concerned about his children. The Father has a special relationship with those who live before him. He counts the hairs on their heads. He knows about their lives and is concerned for them so that it can be stated clearly that he who is God takes care of his children like a Father does. It is very important that the Father and the Son have an intimate relationship. They are time and again referred to in the messages of Paul and of others that the Father and the Son want to give them grace and mercy.

THE FATHER OF THE CRUCIFIED AND RISEN LORD

Luke 10:22 (and Matthew 11:27) already expresses the special relationship between the Father and the Son: "All things have been committed to me by my Father. No one knows who the Son is except the Father, and no one knows who the Father is except the Son and those to whom the Son chooses to reveal him."

The special relationship between Father and Son is expressed in John 5:17, 18, 19, 20–23, 26, 30, 36–37, 43; 6:46; 8:19, 27–28, 38; 10:30; 11:41; 12:27–28, 49; 13:1, 3; 14:8, 9–11, 28, 31; 16:10, 15; and most intensely in John 17.

Jesus' prayer is the climax of the relationship with his Father. He approaches his Father but also prays for his church given to him by his Father. As such, the prayer gains deep significance for the relationship between Father and Son. Beasley-Murray summarizes this well:

> It is of fundamental importance to recognize that in the prayer the basis of the unity of the Church is the nature of God and the reality of his redemptive activity. More specifically, it is an outflow of the relations within the Triune God and of his action in and through the incarnate Son, whereby his saving sovereignty became operative in the world. That unity of God's people became a reality when the Son bestowed on those who believed in him the glory that the Father had given to him (v 22), and it is to find its perfection in the consummation of the saving sovereignty (vv 24–26). The unity of the Church for which Jesus prayed accordingly proceeds from God and belongs essentially to his redemptive work in Christ. As such it transcends all human efforts at reconciling the conflicting interests of people, including those of Christians in their endeavors to harmonize their own interests.[62]

Father and Son are in a very special relationship. The word "glorification" is strongly emphasized, as it is associated with eternal life. The Son glorifies the Father, and the Son is also glorified. This happens for the salvation of man.

The special relationship is unique. Already as a child, Jesus states that he must be busy with the things of his Father, and that the Father entrusts everything to him. The Father does not hide things from Jesus, but entrusts him with these, and his Father can also understand, should it be necessary. In Gethsemane, Jesus pleads for the crucifixion, but submits to the will of God to fulfil the will of God. This truth is also confirmed in Romans 1:7; 15:6; 1 Corinthians 1:3; 8:6; 15:24–28; Philippians 2:11; 1 Timothy 1:2; 2 Timothy 1:2; Hebrews 1:5; 5:5, and 2 John 1:3.

The will of the Father is obvious in the events of the cross. In Gethsemane, Jesus pleads to let the cup bypass him because in those moments he perceives the anxiety and the need of the events of the cross coming upon him. Jesus is deeply grieved and prays to the Father while the disciples do not realize what is happening. He realizes what this is about and pleads the Father to let the cup of suffering bypass him. The events of the cross are the wonder of the new kingdom of God. The kingdom of the cross must

---

62. Beasley-Murray, *John*, 303.

be proclaimed and this can only be done by Jesus in the service of and one with the Father. Turner explains this as follows:

> Matthew 26:39–41. The pathetic cycle occurs three times: Jesus prays alone (26:39, 42, 44; cf. 14:13, 23) but then finds the disciples sleeping instead of staying alert (26:40, 43, 45). As he faces death, his anguish contrasts with their lack of awareness and concern for their master. His prayer in 26:39 (cf. 26:42, 44) expresses his wish to avoid the agonies of the cross, yet he realizes that the Father's plan takes priority over his wishes; the Father's will must be done (6:10; 26:53–54). Jesus portrays his suffering as a cup that must be drunk. His prone posture is in keeping with his submission to the Father (17:6).[63]

Belief in the Father is possible in Jesus Christ the LORD through the Holy Spirit. The wonder of faith is so great that it can not be described and imagined. The beautiful section in John 15 from verse 1 expresses this matter in a special way. The wonder is that forgiveness is possible through the Father who forgives fully in Jesus Christ, the crucified. God's forgiveness shines like a bright light in the darkness when Jesus dies on the cross. God's love is visible, and eternal life is obtained.

The LORD Jesus states that each one will be judged if we do not wholeheartedly forgive our brothers. This also occurs in the Lord's Prayer. One must also forgive others. This is only possible if one believes in Jesus and if his cross becomes a reality in one's life. One can also forgive on account of the cross. In terms of eternal glory and the Father, all honor and glory belong forever to the Father. He is the Father of light, the one who reigns all the time. One must acknowledge his glory, honor, and majesty. True worship of the Father is also extremely important. One can not know God if one does not worship him in spirit and truth. All praise, honor, and thanks belong to the Father, and the believers must still praise God, only when God is known and the Father's glory is confirmed.

---

63. Turner, *Matthew*, 627.

God the Father, Jesus the Son: Love, the Holy Spirit, and Mission

THE UNITY BETWEEN FATHER, Son, and Holy Spirit is important. John 14:16–26 and 15:26 express this as follows: "When the Advocate comes, whom I will send to you from the Father—the Spirit of truth who goes out from the Father—he will testify about me." And Romans 8:15: "The Spirit you received does not make you slaves, so that you live in fear again; rather, the Spirit you received brought about your adoption to sonship. And by him we cry, '*Abba*, Father.'"

The Father, the Son, and the Holy Spirit are most closely linked, thereby confirming the Trinity. As mentioned earlier, the Holy Spirit has a unique effect as a person. The Father, the Son, and the Holy Spirit are also in a very special relationship with each other. Jesus expressly states that the Father, in his name, will send the Advocate, the Holy Spirit, and then the Advocate and the Holy Spirit will do three things: he will testify to sin, righteousness, and judgment in a unique way, in order to highlight the wonder of Jesus Christ. He will be at the right-hand side of God and the Holy Spirit, who is promised and who comes from the Father, and will glorify Christ. The Spirit does not turn people into slaves, but he saves them.

Paul states his discipleship very clearly in terms of the wonder that comes from the Father. Jesus the LORD makes free access to the Father possible. Therefore, one can call out, "Abba, Father!" The believer becomes a child of God who can call to and acknowledge the Father. The Father decided beforehand to choose and link the believers in Christ through the Holy Spirit. They can and must thus be obedient and experience the wonder of eternal life.

The first missional implication of the confession that Jesus is truly one with God is that mission wants to regain transcendence in this reality of secularism and secularity. Transcendence must thus be emphasized based on the confession that Jesus is truly God. His relationship with his Father reveals that he is the one who brings the transcendent God to man. This transcendence means that God can be known in Jesus Christ; this places the presence of God in this reality. The reality is one of falling into sin that makes the meeting of the transcendent God possible. Transcendence is possible because God reveals himself. This reality can thus cause a relationship with God because God reveals himself in Jesus Christ.

In recognition of monotheism, Jesus Christ is revealed as the true person who is present in this world so that God can be made known. Jesus Christ reveals the only true God, and, because this transcendence is possible in Jesus Christ, humans can come into a new relationship with God. Monotheism is thus nonnegotiable in emphasizing God's presence in the world. Mission must live out of this transcendence. Mission must make this the main issue of its confession in the world that God reveals himself in Jesus Christ. This means that one can not simply, for one or other reason, renounce the unique revelation of God in Jesus Christ. God has decided to live within him in his fullness (Col 1). The confession that there is a Triune God is essential for mission. The *missio Trinitatis* is the recognition not simply of a specific mission in the world, but of complete transcendence in which the monotheistic God is acknowledged. Based on this acknowledgment, mission is called to proclaim the confession that Jesus Christ is LORD.

The full glory of Jesus Christ must be recognized in mission. Mission must thus always propagate the fact that Jesus Christ is the transcendent one, whether from a more traditional perspective that proclaims to the people through the church's message that Jesus Christ is LORD or from a more missional perspective of the congregation in the world. He is the one who comes from God. Redemption can only be found in him. Mission will always bear salvation in the meeting of Jesus Christ as the one who is from God and the broken world. One can no longer in this world reason simply on the human level in mission. The tension is too great. Christ is not merely understood on the human level. One can not simply work with people on the level of community organizations. One will have to acknowledge the unity of Jesus Christ with the Father in this time and its extraordinary challenges. Mission must happen from this perspective.

In this world of sin, injustice, disease, and misery, it is meaningless to simply proclaim that Jesus Christ does not really bring about profound changes. He must be proclaimed in the cloud of great witness concerning who he really is. This explains salvation on different levels of life: One must acknowledge Jesus Christ as Son of God, as true Prophet, Priest, and King.

One must acknowledge initiative and stewardship in the economic field but also guard against exploitation. Only once this is acknowledged can salvation also mean something for people in their deepest need. The church must thus live out of this conviction. There is salvation for broken people in the broken Jesus Christ, thus stressing redemption in him. This means that the church moves out into the world. One can experience total redemption only when one acknowledges that Jesus Christ, as the crucified, broken, humble Savior brings salvation.

This also means, however, that one must also seek a new concept of "transcendence." God's transcendence must be confirmed anew in a world in which one lives for the here and now, where theology abandons transcendence for an earthly Jesus who acts here and now. Mission still has a message for the world in which we live, when the full transcendence of God is visible.

It must be very strongly emphasized that Jesus becomes a total man and that he can bring complete redemption and salvation for humans. One must emphasize that reconciliation and redemption take place in Christ. Christ Jesus *is* our reconciliation. His death on the cross creates the possibility of reconciled life with God and of looking forward to sovereignty. This is only possible because Jesus Christ abandons himself. He is the one for the sake of and in place of the other. He abandons himself for the sake of the other; he makes salvation possible in this abandonment of himself as the one for the other. As such, he creates new possibilities of life with God because he is the one on the side of God who abandons himself and on the side of humans because he takes sin upon himself and is made sin. This principle concerning humans' existence is extremely important. Jesus Christ is made to sin, so that he can be the one in whom reconciliation becomes a complete reality. Reconciliation can not be understood in any other way than in Jesus Christ who gives himself as the one for the other. Salvation occurs in the reconciliation which he effects. This means that reconciliation must be understood in very broad terms, including that God's grace is sufficient in Jesus Christ because he is reconciliation. This reaches out to all so that they can all share in it if they are included in the faith of Jesus Christ.

The impossible, however, happens when people die in their sins, separated from God. Jesus Christ is the reconciliation for those who find salvation and redemption in him, who live and die in him. This means that salvation can only be accomplished when one confesses that salvation is *in Christ*. This complete redemption is experienced when one lives with Christ. In his life, in all his different connections, man must find this reconciliation in Christ.

Mission's kerygmatic proclamation must always be that salvation in Christ takes place individually and in community. One can not renounce that salvation is possible in Christ. Mission must fully proclaim that reconciliation is in Christ. Salvation must result in true humaneness. This can only be found when salvation is totally found in Christ. Mission must always convey urgent calls for conversion and devotion to Jesus Christ into the world: "Come, let yourself be reconciled with God," so that this word can be heard. This proclamation always emphasizes, under any circumstance, the free grace of God in Jesus Christ, the LORD (Eph 2:3–10).

If mission does not listen to this, it fails to appreciate the revelation of the monotheistic God, the unity of God, and the special significance of Jesus Christ. Jesus Christ emphasizes true humaneness towards each other, thus the urgent call: "You must love God and thy neighbor."

This implies that the missional church should not fail to appreciate the general understanding of mission. Existence in mission can not be the escape route for the congregation to no longer be involved in conveying the gospel in evangelization. Mission must continue to convey the gospel in its totality. Missionaries are still indispensable to minister the full message of the gospel kerygmatically in the world. Mission is thus more than a conviction or a way of life. Mission means to experience and convey God's great deeds by all possible means and methods.

The Holy Spirit is radically linked to Jesus Christ. Mission can thus emphasize that Jesus is the only LORD. This is the essential principle for the church. From the church, the message is conveyed into the world that he is the LORD. The wonder of Jesus as LORD is not exclusive, but rather inclusive, because he is the LORD who gave his life to all (2 Cor 5).

Mission only has one message: Jesus is the LORD, and the Holy Spirit glorifies him. Only Jesus brings salvation There are three ways in which to establish the relationship with other denominations, namely exclusivism, inclusivism, and pluralism.[1] Exclusivism means that only Jesus can save and

---

1. Crafford, "Teologie van die Godsdienste," 266–70.

that conscious true faith in him is essential. Inclusivism means that only Jesus saves, but that this also takes place anonymously and not everybody knows about this. Pluralism means that Jesus does save, but that this is not unique and that all denominations are equally valid. Van Engen provides an acceptable solution for this by indicating that one must emphasize confession: Jesus Christ is the LORD.[2] This emphasizes the Holy Spirit's confirmation that Jesus is the LORD, that he wants to bring salvation for everyone. This is faith specific. Van Engen summarizes this in a specific way:

> In the evangelist paradigm, confession of Jesus as LORD involves a personal relationship that breaks the bonds of all religious systems. This relationship involves all of life with all its contradictions. It is not neat, logical, coherent. It is not exclusive, nor arrogant, nor triumphalistic. Rather, it is humble confession, repentance and obedience. Thus, the major question is not to what religious system a person belongs. Rather, the crucial issue is one's center. The ultimate question is the question of discipleship, of one's proximity to, or distance from, Jesus the LORD.[3]

It is culturally pluralistic and ecclesiologically inclusive.[4] This message must be impartial; judgment is in God's hands. It is, however, obvious that judgment is not diverted from all people and that the urgent call goes out: Be reconciled with God. Mission may never omit the Holy Spirit's urgent call. It is still the purpose of mission.

Through the Holy Spirit, the church is the space in which one can realize faith in Jesus Christ. Incorporated into the church through baptism, the congregation meets around the word and Holy Communion. The church is the community of love. Love is conveyed to others from the church. True *lived religion* is where Jesus Christ is glorified and the message of his love is conveyed in an impartial manner and does not include general religiosity. It may never be a general mutual-good disposition. The depth of faith, hope, and love is found in Jesus Christ from whom the message must be conveyed to the world. The church can thus be a true missional church. It is the love of the cross of Jesus Christ. The Holy Spirit reveals not only the depth of the death on the cross but also the wonder of life in the cross and in the resurrection. Thus Jesus' urgent call: "The time has come. The kingdom of God has come near. Repent and believe the good news" (Mark 1:15).

2. Van Engen, *Mission on the Way*, 169–85.
3. Van Engen, *Mission on the Way*, 183.
4. Van Engen, *Mission on the Way*, 184, 185.

The Holy Spirit takes care, blesses, and heals. From the wonder of Jesus' grace, the Spirit gives hope under the most horrendous circumstances. During COVID-19, the Holy Spirit who is linked to Jesus gives hope after death. The Christian's true hope is that she/he is more than a victor with the hope of eternal life. The Holy Spirit also brings peace. The Spirit turns spears and swords into agricultural tools, making it possible to avert violence. Jesus brings peace through the Holy Spirit who makes this peace possible. The Holy Spirit is also God's eschatological gift, and therefore hope for the new heaven and new earth is also a reality. The Holy Spirit confirms Jesus' return. One can live with this expectation.

Mission is only possible because the wrath of God is averted in Jesus Christ. The Father is the overabundant fountain of all that is good.[5] It is possible in Jesus Christ through the Holy Spirit to know this wonderful Father and to live as his child. Mission is the powerful movement that introduces this into the world. It has implications for life. God's Fatherhood includes his right. One must thus witness his forgiveness as well as the renewal that comes through him. One must live under the cross as children of God, but one must also live with the expectation that the Father loves us and will make everything new. When one experiences the love of the Father, one can not keep quiet about it. One sees the love of God only in the cross. In his Son, the Father reveals himself most clearly in his love. The resurrection confirms this. This is the heart of mission. All other aspects flow from this. Mission is thus wonderful.

It is, however, extremely important to always prove that the Holy Spirit, the true Spirit of Christ, proclaims the Father's love. The Holy Spirit is the Spirit of truth that guides one in all truth. That truth is Jesus the LORD, the Son of God the Father. The wonder is that the Holy Spirit makes mission possible so that all people and the whole world can experience the fullness of God's love. It must, however, be received through faith effected by the Holy Spirit. Mission can never be separated from the work of the Spirit that empowers the church to help people. The cross of Jesus Christ is at the center of this. Paul wishes to know only the cross of Jesus Christ through the Holy Spirit. The Father confirms this truth in his Son Jesus Christ through the Holy Spirit. Mission emphasizes, realizes, and proclaims the salvation that comes from the Triune God.

Soli deo Gloria

---

5. "Belgic Confession," 1.

BIBLIOGRAPHY

Alfsvåg, Knut. "Postmodern Epistemology and the Mission of the Church." *Mission Studies* 28 (2011) 54–70.
Barrett, C. K. A. *Commentary on the Second Epistle to the Corinthians*. 2nd ed. London: Adam and Charles Black, 1979.
———. *The Gospel According to John: An Introduction with Commentary and Notes on the Greek Text*. London: SPCK, 1976.
———. *Paul: An Introduction to His Thought*. Louisville: Westminster, 1994.
Barr, James. *Bible and Interpretation: The Collected Essays of James Barr. Volume 2: Biblical Studies*. Edited by John Barton. Oxford: Oxford University Press, 2013.
Barth, Karl. *Church Dogmatics. 1/2: The Doctrine of the Word of God: Prolegomena to Church Dogmatics*. Translated by G. T. Thomson and H. Knight. Edinburgh: T. & T. Clark, 1970.
———. *Church Dogmatics. 2/1: The Doctrine of the Word of God*. Edited by G. W. Bromiley and T. F Torrance, translated by T. H. L. Parker et al. Edinburgh: T. & T. Clark, 1957.
———. *Church Dogmatics. 2/2: The Doctrine of God*. Edited by G. W. Bromiley and T. F. Torrance, translated by G. W. Bromiley et al. Edinburgh: T. & T. Clark, 1978.
Barton, John. "Historical Criticism and Literary Interpretation: Is There Any Common Ground?" In *Crossing the Boundaries: Essays in Biblical Interpretation in Honour of Michael D. Goulder*, edited by Stanley. E. Porter et al., 3–16. Leiden: Brill, 1994.
Bavinck, J. H. *An Introduction to the Science of Mission*. Translated by David H. Freeman. Phillipsburg, NJ: Presbyterian and Reformed Press, 1979.
Beasley-Murray, George R. *John*. 2nd ed. Word Biblical Commentary 36. Dallas: Word, 1999.
Bediako, Kwame. "Understanding African Theology in the 20th Century." *Themelios* 20.2 (1994) 14–20.
"Belgic Confession." https://www.crcna.org/welcome/beliefs/confessions/belgic-confession.
Bell, Rob. *Love Wins: At the Heart of Life's Big Questions*. London: Collins, 2011.
Berkhof, H. *Christelijk Geloof: Een Inleiding tot de Geloofsleer*. 2nd ed. Nijkerk, Netherlands: Callenbach, 1973.
Bevans, Stephen B., and Roger P. Schroeder. *Constants in Context: A Theology of Mission for Today*. Maryknoll, NY: Orbis, 2006.
Boer, Roland. *Rescuing the Bible*. Blackwell Manifestos. Malden, MA: Blackwell, 2007.

Bibliography

Bosch, David J. *Transforming Mission: Paradigm Shifts in Theology of Mission*. New York: Orbis, 1991.

Brand, G. V. W. "Witchcraft and Spirit Beliefs in African Christian Theology." *Exchange* 31.1 (2002) 36–50.

Brown, Raymond E. *The Gospel According to John (XIII–XXI)*. London: Chapman, 1972.

———. *The Virginal Conception and Bodily Resurrection of Jesus*. New York: Paulist, 1973.

Bruce, F. F. *The Book of Acts*. Grand Rapids: Eerdmans, 1976.

Burton, Ernest De Witt. "Spirit, Soul, and Flesh: II. רוּחַ, נֶפֶשׁ, and בָּשָׂר in the Old Testament." *The American Journal of Theology* 18.1 (1914) 59–80. https://www.journals.uchicago.edu/doi/10.1086/479314.

Calvin, Jean. *Institusie*. Translated and abridged by Abraham Duvenhage. Potchefstroom, South Africa: Pro Rege, 1967.

———. *Institusie, of Onderwijzing in de Christelijke Godsdienst*. Part 1. Translated by Alexander Sizoo. 3rd impression. Delft: Meinema, 1956.

Collett, Don. "The Christology of Israel's Psalter." *Currents in Theology and Mission* 41.6 (2014) 390–95.

Conradie, Ernst M. "South African Discourse on the Triune God: Some Reflections." *Hervormde Teologiese Studies* 75.1 (2019) 1–11.

Conzelmann, Hans. *Acts of the Apostles: A Commentary on the Acts of the Apostles*. Edited by Eldon J. Epp and Christopher R. Matthews, translated by James Limburg et al. Philadelphia: Fortress, 1987.

Crafford, Dionne. "Teologie van die Godsdienste." In *Suid-Afrika, Land van Baie Godsdienste*, edited by Arno Meiring and Piet Meiring, 210–34. 2nd ed. Wellington, South Africa: CLF, 2015.

Crossan, John Dominic. *The Historical Jesus: The Life of a Mediterranean Jewish Peasant*. Edinburgh: T. & T. Clark, 1991.

———. "The Resurrection of Jesus in Its Jewish Context." *Neotestamentica* 37.1 (2003) 29–57. http://www.jstor.org/stable/43048457.

Crouch, Carly L. *War and Ethics in the Ancient Near East: Military Violence in the Light of Cosmology and History*. Beihefte zur Zeitschrift für die Alttestamentliche Wissenschaft, Band 407. Berlin: De Gruyter, 2009.

Davies, G. H. "The Holy Spirit in the Old Testament." *Review & Expositor* 63.2 (1966) 129–34. https://doi.org/10.1177/003463736606300202.

Dawkins, Richard. *The God Delusion*. London: Black Swan, 2006.

DeClaissé-Walford, Steve G. *Mission as Holistic Ministry: Developing a Congregational Ethos of Community Engagement*. Macon, GA: Smyth & Helwys, 2008.

DeSilva, David A. *An Introduction to the New Testament Contexts, Methods, and Ministry Formation*. Downers Grove: IVP Academic, 2004.

Dingemans, G. D. J. *De Stem van de Roepende: Pneumatologie*. Kampen, Netherlands: Kok, 2000.

Dumbrell. William J. "Spirit and Kingdom of God in the Old Testament." *The Reformed Theological Review* 33.1 (1974) 1–10.

Dunn, James D. G. *Christology in the Making: A New Testament Inquiry into the Origins of the Doctrine of the Incarnation*. 2nd ed. Grand Rapids: Eerdmans, 1989.

Durand, J. J. F. *Die Lewende God*. Wegwysers in die Dogmatiek. Pretoria: NG Kerk-Boekhandel, 1976.

Bibliography

Exalto, K. "Sterven en dan . . . " In *Eschatologie: Handboek over de Christelijke Toekomsverwachting*, edited by W. Van't Spijker, 554–67. Kampen, Netherlands: De Groot Goudriaan, 1999.

Ferdinando, Keith. "Christian Identity in the African Context: Reflections on Kwame Bediako's Theology and Identity." *Journal of the Evangelical Theological Society* 50.1 (2007) 121–43.

Flemming, Dean. *Why Mission?* Edited by Joel B. Green. Reframing New Testament Theology 4. Nashville: Abingdon, 2015.

Fokkelman, J. P. *Reading the Biblical Narrative: An Introductory Guide*. Translated by Ineke Smit. Leiderdorp, Netherlands: Deo, 1999

Freitag, W. *Reden und Aufsätze*. Vol 11. Munich: Chr. Kaiser Verlag, 1961.

Gaffin, Richard B., Jr. "The Holy Spirit." *Westminster Theological Journal* 43.1 (1980) 58–78.

Galli, Mark. *God Wins: Heaven, Hell, and Why the Good News is Better than Love Wins*. Carolstream, IL: Tyndale, 2011.

Ganzevoort, R. Ruard, and Johan Roeland. "Lived Religion: The Praxis of Practical Theology." *International Journal of Practical Theology* 18.1 (2014) 91–101.

Gichaara, K. J. "Issues in African Liberation Theology." *Black Theology* 3.1 (2005) 75–85.

Goheen, Michael W. "A History and Introduction to a Missional Reading of the Bible." In *Reading the Bible Missionally*, edited by Michael W. Goheen, 3–27. Grand Rapids: Eerdmans, 2016.

———. *Introducing Christian Mission Today: Scripture, History and Issues*. Downers Grove: IVP Academic, 2014.

———. "The Missional Church: Ecclesiological Discussion in the Gospel and Our Culture Network in North America." *Missiology: An International Review* 30.4 (2002) 479–90. https://missionworldview.com/wp-content/uploads/2020/06/ea8a85_04b52816d63b4c1eba4fdc841bb41f32.pdf.

Goldingay, John. *Israel's Gospel*. Old Testament Theology 1. Downers Grove: IVP Academic, 2003.

Gorman, Michael J. *Becoming the Gospel: Paul, Participation and Mission*. Grand Rapids: Eerdmans, 2015.

———. "The Interpretation of the Bible in Protestant Churches." In *Scripture: An Ecumenical Introduction to the Bible and Its Interpretation*, edited by Michael J. Gorman, 177–93. Peabody, MA: Hendriksen, 2005.

Gregersen, Niels H. "Deep Incarnation and Kenosis: In, With, Under, and As: A Response to Ted Peters." *Dialog* 52.3 (2013) 251–62.

Guder, Darrell L. *Called to Witness: Doing Missional Theology*. Grand Rapids: Eerdmans, 2015.

Haenchen, Ernst. *John: A Commentary on the Gospel of John, Chapters 7–21*. Translated by Robert W. Funk, edited by Robert W. Funk with Ulrich Busse. Hermeneia: A Critical and Historical Commentary on the Bible. Philadelphia: Fortress, 1984.

Hagner, D. A. *Matthew 1–13*. Word Biblical Commentary 33A. Dallas: Word, 1993.

Hahn, Ferdinand. *Theologie des Neuen Testaments Band 1: Die Vielfalt des Neuen Testaments: Hahn, Theologiegeschichte des Urchristentums*. Tübingen: Mohr Siebeck, 2002.

Harris, Murray J. *The Second Epistle to the Corinthians*. The New International Greek Testament Commentary. Grand Rapids: Eerdmans, 2005.

Hawthorne, Gerald F. *Philippians*. Word Biblical Commentary 43. Dallas: Word, 2004.

Bibliography

Heick, Otto W. *A History of Christian Thought*. Vol 1. Philadelphia: Fortress, 1973.
"Heidelberg Catechism." https://www.crcna.org/welcome/beliefs/confessions/heidelberg-catechism.
Hermans, Christiaan A. M. "From Practical Theology to Practice-Oriented Theology: The Study of Lived Spirituality and Lived Religion in Late Modernity." *International Journal of Practical Theology* 18.1 (2014) 113–26.
Heyns, J. A. *Dogmatiek*. Pretoria: N. G. Kerkboekhandel, 1978.
Heyns, J. A., and W. D. Jonker. *Op Weg met die Teologie*. Pretoria: N. G. Kerkboekhandel, 1974.
Hurtado, L. W. *Lord Jesus Christ: Devotion to Jesus in Earliest Christianity*. Grand Rapids: Eerdmans, 2003.
Hyde, Daniel R. "The Holy Spirit in the Heidelberg Catechism." *Mid-America Journal of Theology* 17 (2006) 211–37. https://www.academia.edu/35514740/The_Holy_Spirit_in_the_Heidelberg_Catechism.
Jasper, David. *A Short Introduction to Hermeneutics*. Louisville: Westminster, 2004.
Jenkins, Paul. "Four Thousand Forgotten Generations: The 'Longue Durée' in African History Challenges: Mission, Theology and Piety." *Mission Studies* 22.2 (2005) 249–65.
Jonker, W. D. *Die Gees van Christus*. Wegwysers in die Dogmatiek. Pretoria: N. G. Kerkboekhandel, 1981.
Joubert, J. "Johannine Metaphors/Symbols Linked to the Paraclete-Spirit and Its Theological Implications." *Acta Theologica* 27.1 (2007) 83–104.
Kaiser, Walter C., Jr. "The Indwelling Presence of the Holy Spirit in the Old Testament." *Evangelical Quarterly* 82.4 (2010) 308–15.
Kärkkäinen, Veli-Matti. *Christ and Reconciliation*. Constructive Christian Theology for the Pluralistic World 1. Grand Rapids: Eerdmans, 2013.
———. *Christology: A Global Introduction*. Grand Rapids: Baker Academic, 2003.
———. *Spirit and Salvation*. Constructive Christian Theology for the Pluralistic World 4. Grand Rapids: Eerdmans, 2016.
Keener, Craig S. *A Commentary on the Gospel of Matthew: A Socio-Rhetorical Commentary*. Grand Rapids: Eerdmans, 1999.
———. *The Gospel of John: A Commentary*. Vol. 1. Grand Rapids: Baker Academic, 2003.
Kennedy, D. J. *Evangelism Explosion*. London: Coverdale House 1973.
Kenzo, Robert, and Mabalia Justin. "Thinking Otherwise about Africa: Postcolonialism, Postmodernism, and the Future of African Theology." *Exchange* 31.4 (2002) 323–41.
Keum, Jooseop, ed. *Together towards Life: Mission and Evangelism in Changing Landscapes—With a Practical Guide*. Geneva: WCC, 2013.
Kim, Kirsteen. "The Holy Spirit in the World: A Global Conversation." *ANVIL* 25.3 (2008) 177–90.
———. "Post-Modern Mission: A Paradigm Shift in David Bosch's Theology of Mission?" *International Review of Mission* 89.353 (2000) 172–79.
Kim, Seyoon. *Paul and the New Perspective: Second Thoughts on the Origin of Paul's Gospel*. Grand Rapids: Eerdmans, 2002.
Kritizinger, J. N. J. "Faith to Faith: Missiology as Encounterology." *Verbum et Ecclesia* 29.3 (2008) 764–90.
Lampe, Peter. "Caesar, Moses and Jesus as 'God', 'Godlike' or 'God's Son': Constructions of Divinity in Paganism, Philo and Christianity in the Greco-Roman World." In *Making*

Bibliography

Sense of Jesus: Experiences, Interpretations and Identities, edited by D. F. Tolmie and R. Venter, 9–27. Bloemfontein, South Africa: Sun Media, 2017.

Lebhar, S. G. "Heaven." In *New Dictionary of Christian Apologetics*, edited by Gavin J. McGrath et al., 295–97. Leicester, UK: Inter-Varsity, 2006.

Liefeld, W. L. "Luke." In *The Expositor's Bible Commentary, Volume 8: Matthew–Luke*, edited by F. E. Gæbelein, 795–1059. Grand Rapids: Zondervan, 1984.

Luz, Ulrich. *Matthew 1–7: A Commentary*. Translated by James E. Crouch. Hermeneia: A Critical and Historical Commentary on the Bible. Minneapolis, MN: Fortress, 2007.

———. *Matthew 21–28: A Commentary*. Edited by Helmut Koester, translated by James E. Crouch. Hermeneia: A Critical and Historical Commentary on the Bible. Minneapolis, MN: Augsburg, 2005.

Macchia, Frank D. "African Enacting Theology: A Rediscovery of an Ancient Tradition?" *Pneuma* 24.2 (2002) 105–09.

Maluleke, Tinyiko Samuel. "Half a Century of African Christian Theologies: Elements of the Emerging Agenda for the Twenty-First Century." *Journal of Theology for Southern Africa* 99 (1997) 4–23.

———. "Identity and Integrity in African Theology: A Critical Analysis." *Religion & Theology* 8.1–2 (2001) 26–41.

Marshall, I. Howard. *New Testament Theology: Many Witnesses, One Gospel*. Downers Grove: InterVarsity, 2004.

Martey, Emmanuel. *African Theology: Inculturation and Liberation*. Maryknoll, NY: Orbis, 1993.

Matthias, M. "'Lutheran' Christology in Barth's Doctrine of Justification." *Zeitschrift für dialektische Theologie* 6 (2014) 12–32.

Mbiti, J. S. *Concepts of God in Africa*. London: SPCK, 1970.

Migliore, Daniel L. *Faith Seeking Understanding: An Introduction to Christian Theology*. Grand Rapids: Eerdmans, 2004.

Moo, Douglas J. *The Epistle to the Romans*. The New International Commentary of the New Testament. Grand Rapids: Eerdmans, 1996.

———. *Galatians*. Baker Exegetical Commentary on the New Testament. Grand Rapids: Baker Academic, 2013.

Moore, E. "Hell." In *New Dictionary of Christian Apologetics*, edited by Gavin J. McGrath et al., 301–05. Leicester: Inter-Varsity, 2006.

Morris, L. *The Gospel According to John*. The New International Commentary on the New Testament. Grand Rapids: Eerdmans, 1984.

Mugambi, Jesse N. K. *African Christian Theology: An Introduction*. Nairobi: East African Educational Press, 1992.

Mukawa, Nzuzi. "Transformation as Missional Goal for Our Churches and Schools." *Direction* 41.2 (2012) 244–51.

Munga, S. I. "Encountering Changes in African Theology." *Svensk Missionstidskrift* 88.2 (2000) 225–50.

Nel, M. J. "The Influence of Dwelling in the Word within the Southern African Partnership of Missional Churches." *Verbum et Ecclesia* 34.1 (2013). http://www.ve.org.za/index.php/VE/article/view/778/1836.

Newbigin, Lesslie. *The Gospel in a Pluralist Society*. Grand Rapids: Eerdmans, 1989.

Ngong, David Tonghou. "God's Will Can Actually Be Done on Earth: Salvation in African Theology." *American Baptist Quarterly* 23.4 (2004) 362–77.

Nicene Creed. https://www.crcna.org/welcome/beliefs/creeds/nicene-creed.

Bibliography

Niemandt, C. J. P. "Acts for Today's Missional Church." *HTS Teologiese Studies/Theological Studies* 66.1 (2010). http://www.hts.org.za/index.php/HTS/article/view/336/76.

———. "Missiology and Deep Incarnation." *Mission Studies* 34.2 (2017) 246–61.

———. "Together Towards New Life for Missiology? Mission and Missiology in the Light of the World Council of Churches 2013 Policy Statement." *Acta Theologica* 35.2 (2015) 82–103.

———. "Trends in Missional Ecclesiology." *HTS Teologiese Studies/Theological Studies* 68.1 (2012).

Nikolajsen. Jeppe Bach. "Missional Church: A Historical and Theological Analysis of an Ecclesiological Tradition." *International Review of Mission* 102.2 (2013) 249.

Nolland, John. *Luke 1:1—9:20*. Word Biblical Commentary 35A. Dallas: Word, 2002.

———. *Luke 9:21—18:34*. Word Biblical Commentary 35B. Dallas: Word, 1993.

Noordegraaf, A. "De eschatologiese prediking van het Nieuwe Testament." In *Eschatologie: Handboek over de Christelijke Toekomsverwachting*, edited by W. Van't Spijker, 85–146. Kampen, Netherlands: De Groot Goudriaan, 1999.

O'Brien, Peter Thomas. *Colossians-Philemon*. Word Biblical Commentary 44. Dallas: Word, 2002.

———. *Gospel and Mission in the Writings of Paul: An Exegetical and Theological Analysis*. Grand Rapids: Baker, 1995.

———. *The Letter to the Hebrews*. Pillar New Testament Commentary. Grand Rapids: Eerdmans, 2010.

Oduyoye, Mercy Amba. *Hearing and Knowing: Theological Reflections on Christianity in Africa*. Eugene, OR: Wipf & Stock, 1986.

Okure, Teresa. "In Him All Things Hold Together: A Missiological Reading of Colossians 1:15-20." *International Review of Mission* 91.360 (2002) 62–72.

O'Neill, William R. "African Moral Theology." *Theological Studies* 62.1 (2001) 122–39.

Pears, Angela. *Doing Contextual Theology*. London: Routledge, 2010.

Pillay, Jerry. "The Missional Renaissance: Its Impact on Churches in South Africa, Ecumenical Organisations, and the Development of Local Congregations." *HTS Teologiese Studies/Theological Studies* 71.3 (2015) http://www.hts.org.za/index.php/HTS/article/view/3065/html.

Pocock, Michael, et al. *The Changing Face of World Missions: Engaging Contemporary Issues and Trends*. Grand Rapids: Baker Academic, 2005.

Quijano, Anibal. "Coloniality and Modernity/Rationality." *Cultural Studies* 21.2–3 (2007) 168–78.

Quijano, Anibal, and Michael Ennis. "Coloniality of Power, Eurocentrism, and Latin America." *Nepantla: Views from South* 1.3 (2000) 533–80.

Saayman, W. A. "If You Were to Die Today, Do You Know for Certain That You Would Go to Heaven?: Reflections on Conversion as Primary Aim of Mission." *Missionalia* 20.3 (1992) 159–73.

Schnabel, E. J. *Early Christian Mission. Vol. 1: Jesus and the Twelve*. Downers Grove: InterVarsity, 2004.

———. *Early Christian Mission. Vol 2: Paul and the Early Church*. Downers Grove: InterVarsity, 2004.

Schreiner, T. R. *The King in His Beauty: A Biblical Theology of the Old and New Testaments*. Grand Rapids: Baker Academic, 2013.

———. *Paul, Apostle of God's Glory in Christ: A Pauline Theology*. Downers Grove: InterVarsity, 2001.

Bibliography

Schweitzer, A. *The Quest for the Historical Jesus: A Critical Study of Its Progress from Reimarus to Wrede*. Translated by W. Montgomery. London: Adam & Charles Black, 1948.

Schweizer, E. *The Letter to the Colossians: A Commentary*. Translated by A. Chester. Minneapolis: Augsburg, 1982.

Setiloane, G. M. *African Theology: An Introduction*. Johannesburg, South Africa: Skotaville, 1986.

Skreslet, S. H. *Comprehending Mission: The Questions, Methods, Themes, Problems, and Prospects of Missiology*. Maryknoll, NY: Orbis, 2012.

Smit, D. *Hoe Verstaan Ons Wat Ons Lees? 'n Dink-en-Werkboek oor die Hermeneutiek, vir Predikers en Studente*. Cape Town, South Africa: NG Kerk-Uitgewers, 1987.

Sutton, Lodewyk. "Clothing Imagery as an Offensive Implement of Warfare and Honour within Psalms 108–110." *Journal for Semitics* 26.1 (2017) 317–39.

Sutton, Lodewyk, and Human, D. J. "'Off with Their Heads!': The Imagery of the Head in the Trilogy of Psalms 108–110, Part 1." *Stellenbosch Theological Journal* 3.1 (2017) 391–410.

Tate, Marvin E. "War and Peacemaking in the Old Testament." *Review & Expositor* 79.4 (1982) 587–96.

Tenney, M. C. "John." In *The Expositor's Bible Commentary Volume 9: John–Acts*, edited by F. E. Gæbelein, 1–206. Grand Rapids: Zondervan, 1981.

Thiselton, A. "Thirty Years of Hermeneutics: Retrospect and Prospects." In *The Interpretation of the Bible*, edited by J Krasovec, 1559–72. Ljubljana, Slovenia: Sheffield, 1998.

Tolmie, D. F. "Discernment in the Letter to the Galatians." *Acta Theologica Supplementum* 17 (2013) 56–171.

Tribe, Reginald. "The Spirit in the Old Testament Writings." *Theology* 32.1191 (1936) 268–69.

Turner, David L. *Matthew*. Baker Exegetical Commentary on the New Testament. Grand Rapids: Baker Academic, 2008.

Van de Beek, A. *Altijd dat Kruis*. Utrecht, Netherlands: Kok Boekencentrum, 2018.

———. *God doet Recht: Eschatologie als Christologie*. Spreken over God 2.1. Zoetermeer, Netherlands: Meinema, 2008.

———. *God Lééft. Over Moeilijke Teksten uit de Bijbel*. Utrecht, Netherlands: Kok Boekencentrum, 2020.

———. *Jezus Kurios: De Christologie als Hart van de theologie*. Spreken over God 1.1. Kampen, Netherlands: Kok, 1998.

———. *De Kring om de Messias: Israël as Volk van de Lijdende Heer*. Spreken over God 1.2. Zoetermeer, Netherlands: Meinema, 2002.

———. *Lichaam en Geest van Christus: De Theologie van de Kerk en de Heilige Geest*. Spreken over God 2.2. Zoetermeer, Netherlands: Meinema, 2012.

———. *Mijn Vader, uw Vader: Het Spreken over God de Vader*. Utrecht, Netherlands: Meinema, 2017.

———. *Schepping: De Wereld als Voorspel voor de Eeuwigheid*. Baarn, Netherlands: Callenbach, 1996.

Van den Berg, Jan-Albert. "Tweeting God: A Practical Theological Analysis of the Communication of Christian Motifs on Twitter." PhD diss., University of Queensland, 2018.

Bibliography

———. "Tweeting God: Finding the Sacred in Everyday Life." Lecture, Faculty of Theology and Religion, University of the Free State, Bloemfontein, South Africa, March 28, 2019.

Van der Walt, B. J. *Understanding and Rebuilding Africa: From Desperation Today to Expectation for Tomorrow*. Potchefstroom, South Africa: Institute for Contemporary Christianity in Africa, 2003.

———. *Visie op die Werklikheid: Die Bevrydende Krag van 'n Christelike Lewensbeskouing en Filosofie*. Potchefstroom, South Africa: PU for CHE, 1999.

Van der Walt, I. J. "Gemeentebou in die Nuwe Afrika." In *Ampsbediening in Afrika*, edited by David J. Bosch, 29–55. Pretoria: NG Kerkboekhandel, 1972.

Van der Westhuizen, Henco. "The Spirit and the Law." *Verbum et Ecclesia* 40.1 (2019) 1–8.

———. "The Trinity in the Canons of Dordt?" *In die Skriflig* 52.2 (2018) 1–9.

———. "The Word and the Spirit: Michael Welker's Theological Hermeneutics, Part 1." *Stellenbosch Theological Journal* 2.2 (2016) 607–20.

———. "The Word and the Spirit: Michael Welker's Theological Hermeneutics, Part 2." *Stellenbosch Theological Journal* 3.1 (2017) 429–49.

Van Engen, Charles. *God's Missionary People: Rethinking the Purpose of the Local Church*. Grand Rapids: Baker, 1991.

———. *Mission on the Way: Issues in Mission Theology*. Grand Rapids: Baker, 1996.

Van Rensburg, Johan Janse. *The Occult Debate: A Scientific and Pastoral Approach*. Cape Town, South Africa: Lux Verbi, 1999.

Venter, R. "Navigating the Plurality of Contemporary Christological Discourses." In *Making Sense of Jesus: Experiences, Interpretations and Identities*, edited by F. Tolmie and R. Venter, 133–50. Bloemfontein, South Africa: Sun Media, 2017.

Vermes, Géza. *The Changing Faces of Jesus*. London: Penguin, 2000.

Verster, Pieter "Abode in Heaven: Paul and Life after Death in 2 Corinthians 5:1–10." *Missionalia* 44.1 (2016) 19–33.

———. "Die Implikasies van die Verlossingsleer van die Marxisme: 'n Sendingkundige Benadering van die Konfrontasie Kerk en Marxisme met Verwysing na die Godsdienskritiek en Verlossingsleer van die Marxisme en Neo-Marxisme." PhD diss., University of Pretoria, 1979.

———. *Jesus Christus, Seun van God, is Ons Versoening: 'n Missionêre Christologie*. Bloemfontein, South Africa: SunMedia, 2017.

———. *New Hope for the Poor*. Bloemfontein, South Africa: SunMedia, 2012.

———. *A Theology of Christian Mission: What Should the Church Seek to Accomplish?* Lewiston, NY: Edwin Mellen, 2008.

———. *Die wonderbare Heilige Gees én die Vader van liefde*. Bloemfontein, South Africa: Sunbonani Scholar, 2020.

Vos, C. J. A. "Die Heilige Gees as Kosmies-Eskatologiese Gawe: 'n Eksegeties-Dogmatiese Studie." PhD diss., University of Pretoria, 1984.

Weaver, J. Denny. *The Non-Violent Atonement*. Grand Rapids: Eerdmans, 2001.

Welker, Michael. *God the Revealed: Christology*. Translated by Douglas W. Stott. Grand Rapids: Eerdmans, 2013.

———. *God the Spirit*. Translated by John F. Hoffmeyer. Minneapolis: Fortress, 1994.

———. "The Spirit in Philosophical, Theological and Interdisciplinary Perspectives." In *The Work of the Spirit, Pneumatology and Pentecostalism*, edited by Michael Welker, 221–32. Grand Rapids: Eerdmans, 2006.

Bibliography

Witherington, Ben, III. *Paul's Letter to Romans: A Socio-Rhetorical Commentary*. Grand Rapids: Eerdmans, 2004.

Wright, Christopher J. H. *The Mission of God: Unlocking the Bible's Grand Narrative*. Nottingham, UK: InterVarsity, 2006.

Wright, N. T. *The Day the Revolution Began: Reconsidering the Meaning of Jesus' Crucifixion*. San Francisco: HarperOne, 2016.

———. *Jesus and the Victory of God*. London: SPCK, 1996.

———. *Paul and the Faithfulness of God: Christian Origins and the Question of God, Parts I and II*. London: SPCK, 2013.

———. *Paul and the Faithfulness of God: Christian Origins and the Question of God, Parts III and IV*. London: SPCK, 2013.

———. *What Saint Paul Really Said: Was Paul of Tarsus the Real Founder of Christianity?* Grand Rapids: Eerdmans, 1997.

Yarbrough, Robert W. *1–3 John*. Baker Exegetical Commentary on the New Testament. Grand Rapids: Baker Academic, 2008.

Subject Index

Africa, 52, 53, 54, 55, 96, 97, 98
ancestors, 45, 96
ascension, 58, 66, 84, 99
atonement, 19, 20, 22, 61, 77, 103

belief, 14, 15, 19, 40, 74, 80, 134
birth, 53, 58, 59, 66, 105

Christology, 11, 16, 19, 24, 25, 27, 29,
 35, 37, 39, 41, 44, 49, 57, 58, 62, 68
church, 1, 2, 4, 8, 9, 10, 11, 12, 13, 14,
 16, 18, 25, 27, 30, 46, 48, 49, 53, 54,
 55, 56, 60, 61, 64, 67, 68, 69, 72, 73,
 87, 88, 89, 91, 92, 94, 95, 96, 97, 98,
 99, 100, 102, 107, 110, 113, 117,
 124, 130, 133, 137, 138, 139, 140
colonialism, 52, 53
cosmological, 68, 69, 86, 87, 88, 90, 91,
 94, 95, 96, 99
creation, 3, 5, 6, 12, 15, 16, 38, 40, 41,
 49, 50, 51, 54, 58, 78, 88, 89, 90, 91,
 93, 94, 99, 109, 110, 114, 115, 116
cross, 14, 16, 36, 37, 38, 39, 48, 49, 50,
 54, 55, 58, 59, 60, 61, 62, 78, 79,
 82, 83, 85, 103, 104, 109, 122, 123,
 126, 127, 128, 129, 130, 131, 133,
 134, 137, 139, 140
crucifixion, 34, 60, 61, 76, 83, 133

discipleship, 123, 135, 139

economy, 51, 55
evangelization, 10, 15, 138

Father, 5, 10, 14, 17, 22, 26, 29, 32, 34,
 35, 37, 38, 41, 43, 44, 46, 60, 68, 73,
 74, 76, 79, 80, 83, 84, 90, 95, 99,
 101, 102, 103, 104, 106, 109, 110,
 117, 118, 119, 120, 121, 122, 123,
 124, 125, 128, 129, 131, 132, 133,
 134, 135, 136, 140

God, 1, 3, 4, 6, 8, 9, 10, 11, 12, 14, 16,
 17, 19, 20, 21, 22, 23, 25, 26, 27, 28,
 29, 30, 31, 32, 33, 34, 35, 36, 37, 38,
 39, 40, 41, 42, 44, 45, 46, 47, 48, 49,
 50, 51, 54, 55, 56, 57, 58, 59, 60, 61,
 62, 64, 65, 66, 67, 68, 69, 70, 71, 72,
 74, 77, 78, 79, 80, 81, 82, 83, 84, 86,
 87, 88, 89, 90, 91, 93, 94, 95, 96, 99,
 101, 102, 103, 104, 105, 106, 107,
 108, 109, 110, 111, 112, 113, 114,
 115, 116, 117, 118, 119, 120, 121,
 122, 123, 124, 125, 126, 127, 128,
 129, 130, 131, 132, 133, 134, 135,
 136, 137, 138, 139, 140

heaven, 9, 14, 35, 37, 44, 50, 64, 65, 67,
 89, 91, 103, 109, 117, 120, 121,
 122, 124, 125, 126, 127, 128, 129,
 132, 140
hell, 64, 65, 126, 127
hermeneutic, 1, 7, 8, 29, 31, 65, 98
Holy Spirit, 3, 4, 5, 6, 8, 10, 11, 13, 14,
 15, 17, 18, 40, 58, 68, 69, 70, 71, 72,
 73, 74, 75, 76, 77, 78, 79, 80, 81, 82,
 83, 84, 85, 86, 87, 88, 89, 90, 92, 93,

Subject Index

(Holy Spirit continued)
  94, 95, 96, 98, 99, 100, 101, 102, 103, 104, 105, 106, 107, 108, 109, 110, 111, 112, 113, 115, 116, 118, 119, 131, 134, 135, 138, 139, 140

Jesus Christ, 1, 2, 4, 6, 8, 13, 14, 15, 17, 18, 19, 20, 21, 22, 23, 25, 26, 27, 28, 29, 30, 31, 33, 34, 35, 36, 38, 39, 40, 46, 47, 48, 52, 55, 56, 58, 59, 61, 62, 66, 67, 68, 76, 78, 79, 80, 84, 85, 86, 89, 92, 99, 103, 104, 107, 110, 111, 112, 113, 114, 118, 119, 123, 125, 126, 127, 130, 131, 134, 135, 136, 137, 138, 139, 140
judgement, 23

king, 20, 32, 36, 43, 44, 46, 70, 113, 137

lived religion, 73, 139
Logos, 37, 45, 58, 59
Lord's prayer, 119, 120, 121, 122, 123, 124, 134
love, 10, 13, 14, 15, 16, 17, 18, 22, 40, 48, 60, 62, 65, 66, 68, 69, 80, 81, 95, 103, 104, 107, 111, 113, 117, 118, 119, 123, 124, 125, 126, 127, 129, 130, 131, 132, 134, 135, 138, 139, 140

mediation, 107
Mediator, 37, 38, 41, 60, 62, 73, 76, 96
missio Dei, 9, 10, 11, 12
mission, 1, 5, 6, 8, 9, 10, 11, 12, 13, 14, 15, 16, 17, 18, 20, 29, 34, 42, 43, 46, 48, 49, 50, 51, 52, 54, 55, 56, 57, 58, 62, 67, 68, 69, 72, 73, 75, 76, 77, 78, 79, 91, 98, 99, 100, 104, 110, 117, 119, 125, 136, 137, 138, 139, 140
missional, 11, 12, 13, 16, 61, 64, 65, 67, 68, 136, 138, 139
missiones ecclesiae, 10
monotheism, 27, 28, 29, 30, 44, 103, 136

Offices, 43
ordo salutis, 109

pacifist, 49, 82

patriarchal, 117
patrology, 117
Pentecost, 93, 105
politics, 48
postcolonial, 52, 53, 54, 55
Postmodernism, 5
priest, 20, 56, 57, 61, 137
prophet, 20, 35, 36, 45, 46, 47, 55, 56, 58, 137
Protestants, 87

reconciliation, 16, 19, 46, 49, 51, 56, 57, 60, 62, 66, 67, 69, 78, 104, 108, 137, 138
redemption, 5, 6, 11, 14, 15, 16, 17, 28, 32, 34, 35, 43, 44, 47, 50, 56, 57, 58, 61, 64, 65, 66, 67, 78, 80, 81, 82, 90, 98, 104, 110, 111, 112, 114, 115, 116, 123, 126, 127, 129, 130, 131, 136, 137, 138
resurrection, 3, 15, 28, 35, 36, 38, 39, 40, 56, 59, 61, 62, 63, 64, 66, 74, 81, 103, 115, 130, 131, 140
return, 13, 58, 66, 103, 125, 140
revelation, 2, 3, 4, 5, 6, 8, 9, 19, 23, 25, 27, 33, 37, 38, 66, 72, 74, 75, 86, 87, 90, 95, 103, 118, 136, 138
ruach, 69, 70, 72, 90, 95, 99, 106

salvation, 10, 12, 13, 14, 15, 16, 17, 23, 25, 26, 28, 29, 30, 34, 35, 37, 38, 40, 41, 44, 46, 47, 48, 49, 50, 51, 55, 56, 57, 58, 59, 61, 62, 63, 64, 65, 66, 67, 68, 69, 73, 80, 83, 84, 88, 89, 90, 93, 103, 104, 109, 110, 111, 112, 113, 114, 119, 122, 124, 126, 131, 136, 137, 138, 139, 140
science, 49, 50
scripture, 2, 3, 4, 5, 6, 7, 8, 12, 21, 22, 25, 26, 31, 42, 54, 65, 72, 76, 86, 87, 95, 119
sin, 13, 15, 16, 28, 49, 54, 61, 62, 64, 66, 67, 68, 75, 76, 77, 78, 79, 82, 83, 87, 88, 94, 104, 108, 112, 113, 115, 122, 123, 124, 127, 135, 136, 137
Son, 10, 14, 15, 17, 19, 20, 21, 22, 24, 25, 28, 29, 30, 31, 32, 33, 34, 35, 36, 37, 38, 40, 41, 42, 44, 45, 56, 58, 59,

Subject Index

60, 62, 67, 73, 74, 77, 84, 90, 95, 99, 101, 102, 103, 104, 109, 113, 114, 118, 119, 128, 129, 132, 133, 135, 137, 140

sovereignty, 20, 21, 23, 34, 38, 55, 66, 102, 119, 133, 137

Spirit, 3, 4, 5, 6, 8, 10, 11, 13, 14, 15, 17, 18, 22, 37, 40, 58, 59, 61, 63, 68, 69, 70, 71, 72, 73, 74, 75, 76, 77, 78, 79, 80, 81, 82, 83, 84, 85, 86, 87, 88, 89, 90, 91, 92, 93, 94, 95, 96, 97, 98, 99, 100, 101, 102, 103, 104, 105, 106, 107, 108, 109, 110, 111, 112, 113, 114, 115, 116, 118, 119, 121, 131, 134, 135, 138, 139, 140

suffering, 2, 20, 28, 46, 48, 50, 55, 60, 61, 62, 65, 78, 84, 118, 130, 131, 133, 134

technology, 50, 51

temptation, 121, 123

theology, 1, 2, 3, 8, 12, 16, 23, 27, 36, 38, 39, 41, 52, 53, 54, 55, 61, 68, 79, 87, 88, 89, 91, 92, 93, 97, 98, 114, 130, 137

Trinity, 5, 68, 69, 70, 72, 84, 89, 99, 100, 101, 102, 103, 104, 107, 118, 135

Triune God, 4, 8, 12, 17, 51, 55, 95, 118, 119, 133, 136, 140

virginal conception, 58

YHWH, 25, 27, 30, 31, 32, 36, 40, 43, 44, 46, 70, 121

Scripture Index

GENESIS
1:1–2	70, 90, 91, 99
12	131
15	131
21:20	71
22	131
26:3	71

NUMBERS
15:30–31	77

DEUTERONOMY
6:4	44
18:5	57
29:18–20	77

2 SAMUEL
23:2	90

JOB
29:15–17	81

PSALMS
1	32
2	32
8:3	90
16	35
102:28	32
110	35
147:10–11	81

PROVERBS
1:20–23	34
8:1–36	34

ISAIAH
2:4	81
63:10	71

HAGGAI
2:1	77

MATTHEW
1:22	58
3:11–12	33
3:17	34
4:23	59
5	47
6:9–10	119
6:10	134
6:26	132
7:21	128
8:12	65
10:7–8	15
10:29	132
10:33	128
11:25–30	33
12:18	34
12:31–32	77
13:40–43	120
14:12; 23	134
16:27–28	120

Scripture Index

(Matthew continued)

17:5	34
17:6	134
19:28–30	120
25:30	65
25:34	120
26:19–20	77
26:39–45; 53–54	134
26:45	65
28:10–20	77
28:18	33
28:18–19	8, 34
28:19	101
28:19–20	15

MARK

1:1	34, 37
1:15	139
9:43, 48	65
14:24	34
15:33	34, 39

LUKE

4:18	35
10:22	132
10:38	35
13:10–17	80
13:28	65
15:11–32	124–5
16:23	65

JOHN

1:1–2	23, 32, 99
6:37	14
6:51, 58	32
6:53–58	14
8:34	15
14:1–4	14
14:6	74, 83
16:7–13	75, 83
16:8	76
16:11	80
16:14	84
16:14–16	88
18:38	83

ACTS

1:3, 8	15
2:32–36	35
7:55	36
9:5	36
10:39–43	36
13:32–37	36
16:31	36
17:23–31	36
26:15	36
32:8	36
28:30–31	36

ROMANS

1:20	90
1:4	40
2:29	114
3:21	40
3:25	40
5	66
5:1	40
5:5	114
5:10	62
6:4	40
6:5–8	62, 63
7:6	114
6:23	40
8:2–16	114
8:15	118
8:17	40
8:17; 18–25	114, 115
8:17–25	115
8:22–27	115
8:39	40
8:9	73
8:26	113
9:5	40
11:33–36	41
14:9	41
15:7–13	41
15:9	41

1 CORINTHIANS

1:3	133
2:10–16	107
8:6	133

Scripture Index

15:12–19	64
15:22	104
15:24–28	133
15:44	63

2 CORINTHIANS

5	138
5:1–10	14
5:11	104
5:11–21	61, 62
5:19–21	83
6:18	131
12:1–10	80

GALATIANS

4:23; 29	106
5:17; 16–26	111

EPHESIANS

2:1–3	62
2:3–10	138
6	123

PHILIPPIANS

2:5–11	37
2:6–11	25, 39
2:11	133

COLOSSIANS

1	136
1:15–20	32, 41

1 TIMOTHY

1:2	133
3:16	37

2 TIMOTHY

1:2	133

HEBREWS

1:1–4	37
1:5	133
5:5	133
6:6	77
9:8	106
10:31	14
12:7–9	129

1 PETER

1:3; 23	106

1 JOHN

3:9; 24	113

2 JOHN

1:3	133

JUDE

13	65

REVELATIONS

1:4; 8	32
4	103
4–5	120
4:8	121
19:20	65
20:14	65
21:8	65
22:17	103

www.ingramcontent.com/pod-product-compliance
Lightning Source LLC
Chambersburg PA
CBHW051936160426
43198CB00013B/2177